DOON MACKICHAN

Doon Mackichan studied drama at Manchester University and has since worked extensively in theatre, radio, television and film. As an actress her theatre credits include *The Queen and I* (Royal Court); *A Midsummer Night's Dream* (Almeida / tour) and *Mother Courage* (Royal National Theatre).

For television she is best known as one of the writers and performers in *Smack the Pony*, awards for which include an Emmy, an Indy and a Bamft. Other credits include *Brass Eye*, *Our Mutual Friend*, *Knowing Me, Knowing You* with Alan Partridge, and *The Day Today*.

Her writing credits for radio include *Doon Your Way* and *Rabbitt and Doon*, both for Radio 4. Her film work includes *The Borrowers*, *Thanks for the Memories* and *Old New Borrowed Blue*.

Doon lives in London and is married with two children.

MARTIN MILLAR

Martin Millar was born in Glasgow but has lived for more than twenty years in South London. His first novel *Milk, Sulphate and Alby Starvation,* was published in 1987. Since then he has written five more novels: *Lux the Poet*; *Ruby and the Stone Age Diet*; *The Good Fairies of New York*; *Dreams of Sex and Stage Diving*; and *Love and Peace with Melody Paradise*.

He has also written a graphic novel, *Lux and Alby Sign on and Save the Universe*, and was responsible for the novelisation of the film *Tank Girl*.

His web site can be found at www.martinmillar.com

Emma

adapted from Jane Austen's novel by

**Martin Millar
and
Doon Mackichan**

NICK HERN BOOKS

London

www.nickhernbooks.co.uk

A Nick Hern Book

This adaptation of Emma first published in Great Britain
in 2001 as an original paperback by Nick Hern Books Limited,
14 Larden Road, London W3 7ST

Emma © 2001 by Martin Millar and Doon Mackichan

Martin Millar and Doon Mackichan have asserted their right
to be identified as the authors of this work

Front cover photo copyright © Geoff Brightling

Typeset by Country Setting, Kingsdown, Kent CT14 8ES
Printed and bound in Great Britain by Biddles of Guildford

A CIP catalogue record for this book is available from the
British Library

ISBN 185459 499 0

Notes on the Play

Our Inspiration

Jane Austen often wrote at night, her only real privacy, and spent much of her day looking after a myriad of nephews and nieces. She guarded her manuscripts and only when finished did she sometimes allow them to be acted out by her young relatives in a sitting room or barn, Jane often taking the part of the leading man.

As our play begins, it is night and an exhausted Jane Austen sleeps over the recently completed manuscript of her new novel, *Emma*. Four of her young nieces steal on stage and after some quarrelling decide to purloin the text and act it out. Jane is awakened and after her initial anger, allows the girls to begin to tell her story. Irritated by the absurd posturings of one niece playing Mr Knightley, Jane Austen takes this role and keeps it whilst the real Emma and Mr Wodehouse enter, the nieces providing the many other characters. These excitable teenage girls often try to take the story into their own realms of fantasy but are always brought back to the real text by Jane.

The nieces in effect perform the show, each taking mostly one main part for themselves. They never leave the stage but sit on benches behind the area where the action unfolds. They provide an energetic vocal and physical chorus to support the story, never upstaging, always alert and always slightly in awe of their 'Aunty Jane'. They are the show's life-blood, and their energy (on the cusp of puberty, full of sexual tension and excitement) drives the show. Their costumes are period with attitude – Empire-Line dresses fall open to reveal the girls wearing modern pedal-pushers and trainers, allowing them the freedom of movement to be at once feminine and tomboyish – one minute they dance wildly to the Prodigy, the next they execute a perfect Scottish reel.

The Set

Ideally the actors create the pictures in a dynamic ensemble performance. Therefore the set can be minimal, with three benches and an old toy box, from which come the props, normally one per character (i.e. for Mrs Elton a feather boa, Mrs Bates a lace hat, Jane Fairfax a volume of Proust). While sitting on the benches, the nieces would usually act as a chorus and commentary on the proceedings, before invading the stage to play their other characters.

Jane Austen

We were very keen for the same actress to portray Jane Austen and Mr Knightley because we felt that a lot of Jane Austen's voice is in this ideal man. This doubling can be easily achieved with a clever costume design (we used a long frock coat and leather boots – both masculine and feminine) and with the simple putting on of glasses to signify the change between Jane Austen and Mr Knightley, in addition to the obvious physical and vocal transformation. She remains on stage at all times, watching her book unfold, guiding the nieces, and seeing her heroine undergo her painful journey. She can be as close to or as far from the action as your production requires but she is always our simultaneous narrator and commentator.

House Style

There is a rebellious bold spirit to the piece – it is physical, truthful, moving and funny. It is the essence of Austen – caustic, dark, but ultimately forgiving. As Jane Austen said 'Pictures of perfection, as you know, make me sick and wicked.'

Our actors don't have much rest, they comment vocally and physically throughout the show. Quick changes are vital to the spirit of the show, particularly Woodhouse who goes from leering vicar to lusty farmer to valetudinarian, often without pause. With so much happening on stage it is essential to keep a focus, and the nieces are integral to this. (Emma and Frank

Churchill are the only characters who just play themselves. It is as if they are from another world.)

Remember that this is simply a guide. Stick to the text but reinterpret it as you wish. That pertains to the music and the stage directions as well. It is fast, witty and vibrant and populated with real people, and that is the point, they are real people. It is a modern reworking, but despite our occasional irreverence, the wit and genius of Jane Austen must shine through.

Doon MacKichan
Martin Millar

Emma was first presented at the Gilded Balloon Theatre during the 1998 Edinburgh Festival and subsequently on a tour which included Watford Palace Theatre before transferring in October 1999 to the the Tricycle Theatre, London. The original cast was as follows:

EMMA	Doon MacKichan
JANE AUSTEN / MR KNIGHTLEY	Nicola Redmond
NIECE ONE / MISS BATES	Gillian Hannah
NIECE TWO / JANE FAIRFAX	Lucy Briers
NIECE THREE / MRS WESTON / MRS ELTON	
	Abigail McKern
NIECE FOUR / HARRIET SMITH	Lucy Scott
FRANK CHURCHILL	Adam Croasdell
MR ELTON / MR WOODHOUSE / ROBERT MARTIN / MRS COLES	Michael Matthus

Other characters played by members of the company

Director Guy Retallack
Designer Dora Schweitzer

Characters

JANE AUSTEN

EMMA

MR KNIGHTLEY

HARRIET SMITH

ROBERT MARTIN

FRANK CHURCHILL

JANE FAIRFAX

MRS WESTON

MR ELTON

MRS ELTON

MRS COLES

MISS BATES

MR WOODHOUSE

MISS BICKERTON

NIECE ONE

NIECE TWO

NIECE THREE

NIECE FOUR

For ideal doubling, see cast list on previous page

Scene 1

JANE AUSTEN *is asleep centre stage. All four nieces enter and perform a rap dance to the music of Me'Shell's 'If that's your boyfriend'.*

NIECES. You say that's your boyfriend,
    You say I'm out of line,
    Funny . . . he said I could call him up anytime.

    You could call me wrong, say that I ain't right
    But if that's your boyfriend he wasn't last night.

    Now I'm the kind of woman,
    I'll do almost anything to get what I want.
    I might play any little game.
    Call me what you like but you know what to do.
    You're just jealous, cos he wasn't with you.

    I don't mean no harm. I just like what I see
    And it ain't my fault, if he wants me.

    That's what I want, and the feeling was right.
    If that's your boyfriend he wasn't last night.

    Boyfriend, yes I had your boyfriend.

    If that's your boyfriend, if that's your boyfriend,
    If that's your boyfriend he wasn't last night!

The music comes to a rude halt when they discover JANE AUSTEN *in the room. One of them is brave enough to steal the book she is working on. She reads.*

NIECE ONE (*sotto voce*). Emma Woodhouse, handsome, clever, rich, with a comfortable home and happy disposition, seemed to unite some of the best blessings of existence: and had lived nearly twenty-one years in the world with very little to distress or vex her.

NIECE TWO. She dearly loved her father, but he was no companion for her. He could not meet her in conversation, rational or playful; for having been a vale . . . vale . . .

NIECE ONE. Valetudinarian.

NIECE TWO. . . . all his life, without activity of mind or body, he was a much older man in ways than in years; and though everywhere beloved for the friendliness of his heart and his amiable temper, his talents could not have recommended him at any time.

All look depressed at prospect of a dull novel.

NIECE THREE. They lived in Highbury, (*Squeals of delight from the other nieces.*) a large and populous village, amounting to a town, to which Hartfield, in spite of its separate lawns and shrubberies and name, did really belong. The Woodhouses were first in consequence there. All looked up to them.

NIECE FOUR. Is there a handsome hero?

NIECE ONE (*flicking through pages of novel*). Yes . . . Mr Knightley.

The nieces quarrel about who is to play MR KNIGHTLEY.

NIECES. I'm him . . . no I am . . . no I'm him . . . no, me . . . me . . . me etc.

NIECE TWO (*beginning tentatively and then growing in confidence*). Ah, Mr Woodhouse! Delightful to see you! It is a beautiful moonlit night, is it not? Delightful to see you! A beautiful moonlit night is it not? I say, did you ever see a more beautiful moonlit night? I must say, it is a . . .

JANE AUSTEN (*having woken*). What are you doing?

NIECES *recoil.*

NIECE ONE (*slightly sulky having just been caught out*). Just playing.

JANE AUSTEN. With my book? My new book?

NIECE FOUR. We just wanted to know the story Auntie Jane. Sorry.

Ominous pause.

JANE AUSTEN. It's all right.

NIECES *sit down round* JANE AUSTEN *and she hands the book to* NIECE TWO.

Go on then.

NIECE TWO (*resuming* MR KNIGHTLEY *but a little subdued*). Ah! Mr Woodhouse! Delightful to see you! It is a beautiful moonlit night, is it not? Delightful to see you! (*Starting to overblow the character to the delight of the other giggling nieces.*) Did you ever see a more beautiful moonlit night? Ah!

JANE AUSTEN. Mr Knightley is not a brainless coxcomb! Mr Knightley is like . . . like . . . this.

JANE AUSTEN *becomes* MR KNIGHTLEY. NIECE ONE *becomes* MR WOODHOUSE.

NIECE ONE (*as confident young man*). It is very kind of you, Mr Knightley to come out at this late hour to call upon us. (NIECE TWO *tells him he should play it old.*) I am afraid you must have had a shocking walk.

MR KNIGHTLEY. Not at all, Sir. It is a beautiful moonlit night, and so mild that I must draw back from your great fire.

NIECE ONE. But you must have found it very damp and dirty. I wish you may not catch cold.

MR KNIGHTLEY. Dirty, Sir? Look at my boots. Not a speck on them.

NIECE ONE. Well that is quite surprising for we have had a vast deal of rain here. I wanted them to put off the wedding. Ah, poor Miss Taylor, it is a sad business.

NIECE THREE *and* FOUR (*to* JANE AUSTEN). Who's Miss Taylor?

JANE AUSTEN. Miss Taylor was Emma's governess. She just got married today to a Mr Weston.

NIECE ONE. Poor Miss Taylor.

MR KNIGHTLEY. Poor Emma and Mr Woodhouse if you please, for you will sorely miss her, but I cannot possibly say poor Miss Taylor. It must be easier for Miss Taylor to have only one to please rather than two.

NIECE FOUR. Emma! Who's playing Emma?

NIECE THREE *and* FOUR *discuss whom of the two of them would be better for the part but are superseded by*

NIECE TWO. *The next two speeches are simultaneously read by the nieces and the real* EMMA *and* MR WOODHOUSE *as they appear from the audience.*

NIECE TWO / EMMA (*fading in*). . . . especially when one of those two is such a fanciful troublesome creature. That is what you have in your head, I know, and what you would certainly say if my father were not by.

MR WOODHOUSE / NIECE ONE (*fading out*). I believe it is very true, my dear, indeed. I am afraid I am sometimes very fanciful and troublesome.

NIECE ONE *and* TWO *re-take their seats on the bench with the other* NIECES.

EMMA. My dearest papa, you do not think I could mean you, or suppose Mr Knightley to mean you. What a horrible idea! Oh, no, I meant only myself. Mr Knightley loves to find fault with me, you know – in a joke – it is all in a joke. We always say what we like to one another. And have you forgotten, papa, one matter of joy to me, that I made the match myself. I made the match four years ago and to have it take place and be proved in the right, when so many people said Mr Weston would never marry again, may comfort me for anything.

MR WOODHOUSE. Ah, my dear Emma, I wish you would not make matches and foretell things, for whatever you say always comes to pass. Pray do not make any more matches.

EMMA. I promise to make none for myself, but I must indeed for other people. It is the greatest amusement in the world. Everybody said that Mr Weston would never marry again but I believed none of it. I planned the match and I was blessed with success.

MR KNIGHTLEY. I do not understand what you mean by success. Success supposes endeavour. You made a lucky guess and that is all that can be said.

MR WOODHOUSE. Emma never thinks of herself if she can do good to others, but my dear, pray, do not make any more matches. They are silly things and break up one's family circle grievously.

EMMA. Only one more papa. Only for Mr Elton. Poor Mr
Elton. I must look about for a wife for him.

NIECES *all applaud* EMMA.

Scene 2

JANE AUSTEN. Miss Harriet Smith was a girl of seventeen
whom Emma knew very well by sight and had long felt an
interest in, on account of her beauty.

All nieces stretch their hands up to be picked. JANE
AUSTEN *puts her hand on the shoulder of* NIECE FOUR
who becomes HARRIET.

EMMA (*to audience and circling* HARRIET). I am not struck
by anything remarkably clever in Miss Smith's
conversation, but I find her altogether very engaging,
showing so proper and becoming a deference, seemingly so
pleasantly grateful for being admitted to Hartfield, and so
artlessly impressed by the appearance of everything in so
superior a style to what she had been used to, that she must
have good sense and deserve encouragement. These soft
blue eyes and all those natural graces should not be wasted
on the inferior society of Highbury. The friends, for whom
she had just parted, though a very good sort of people, must
be doing her harm. They were a family of the name of
Martin. They must be coarse and unpolished and very unfit
to be the intimates of Harriet Smith. I will notice her, I will
improve her, I will detach her from bad acquaintance and
introduce her into good society. I will inform her opinion
and her manners. It will be an interesting and certainly a
very kind undertaking. (*To* HARRIET.) What sort of a
looking man is Mr Martin?

They begin to walk down the road.

HARRIET. Oh, not handsome, not at all handsome. I thought
him very plain at first but I do not think him so plain now.
One does not, you know, after a time. But did you never see
him? He has passed you very often.

EMMA. That may be and I have seen him fifty times, but without having any idea of his name. A young farmer is the very last sort of person to raise my curiosity. A degree or two lower and I might hope to be useful to his family, but a farmer can need none of my help and is therefore in one sense as much above my notice as in every other he is below it.

They meet MR MARTIN *on the road.*

HARRIET. Hello Mr Martin.

ROBERT MARTIN. Hello Miss Smith. Miss Woodhouse.

He exits.

HARRIET. Think of us happening to meet him. How very odd. He's been out looking for walnuts for me.

EMMA. In December?

HARRIET. Well, that's what he said. Tell me, Miss Woodhouse, is he what you expected? What do you think of him? Do you think him so very plain?

EMMA. He is very plain, undoubtedly – remarkably plain, but that is nothing compared to his entire want of gentility. I did not expect much, but I had no idea that he could be so very clownish, so totally without air. I had imagined him a degree or two nearer gentility.

HARRIET. To be sure, he is not so genteel as a real gentleman.

EMMA. Harriet, since your acquaintance with us you have been repeatedly in the company of some such very real gentlemen. You must be struck with the difference in Mr Martin. What will he be in a few years?

HARRIET. There is no saying indeed.

EMMA. There is pretty good guessing. He will be a completely gross, vulgar farmer – totally inattentive to appearances, and thinking of nothing but profit and loss.

HARRIET. But these are important things, Miss Woodhouse.

MR ELTON *enters.*

JANE AUSTEN. Mr Elton was the very person fixed on by Emma for driving the young farmer out of Harriet's head. Mr Elton had a comfortable home for her at the Vicarage of

Highbury, he was reckoned very handsome, and the girl who could be gratified by a Robert Martin's riding about the country for her, might very well be conquered by Mr Elton's admiration.

EMMA (*whispering to* HARRIET). Curtsey!!

HARRIET *curtseys to* MR ELTON, *giggles and rushes off.*

MR ELTON. You have given Miss Smith all that she required; you have made her graceful and easy. She was a beautiful creature when she came to you, but in my opinion the attractions you have added are infinitely superior to what she received from nature.

EMMA. I am glad you think I have been useful to her, but Harriet only wanted drawing out. She had all the natural grace of sweetness of temper and artlessness in herself. I have done very little.

MR ELTON. If it were admissible to contradict a lady . . .

EMMA. I have perhaps given her a little more decision of character, and taught her to think on points, which had not fallen in her way before.

MR ELTON. Exactly so – skilful has been the hand.

EMMA. Great has been the pleasure I'm sure. I never met with a disposition more truly amiable.

MR ELTON. I have no doubt of it. Will you be going to the Coles' dinner party?

EMMA. No, I am afraid not.

MR ELTON. Oh, what a pity. Well, I must be off now. So nice to . . . well . . . good-bye.

EMMA (*miming to audience*). YES!!

Scene 3

JANE AUSTEN *is asleep.*

NIECE ONE. Harriet receives a letter.

NIECE TWO (*as* POSTMAN). Letter for Miss Smith.

The NIECES *run in a flurry behind* HARRIET *who tears around the stage at great speed.*

NIECE ONE. The letter was from him, from Robert Martin, and contained a direct proposal of marriage.

NIECE TWO. Who could have thought it, she was so surprised she did not know what to do.

NIECE THREE. Yes, quite a proposal of marriage.

NIECE ONE. And it was a very good letter, at least she thought so.

NIECE TWO. And he wrote as if he really loved her very much.

NIECE ONE. So she has come as fast as she could so she could ask Miss Woodhouse what should she do.

HARRIET (*running and calling*). Miss Woodhouse! Miss Woodhouse! (HARRIET *face to face with* EMMA.) Will you read the letter, pray do, I'd rather you would.

JANE AUSTEN *awakens.*

JANE AUSTEN. Emma was not sorry to be pressed. She read and was surprised. The style of the letter was much above her expectations. As a composition it would not have disgraced a gentleman. The language, though plain, was strong and unaffected. It was short, but it expressed good sense, warm attachment, liberality, even delicacy of feeling.

HARRIET. Well, is it a good letter, or is it too short?

During the next speech a certain amount of sexual excitement rises in EMMA.

EMMA. Yes, indeed, a very good letter, so good a letter, Harriet, that everything considered, I think one of his sisters must have helped him. I can hardly imagine that the young man could express himself so well if left quite to his own powers. (EMMA *looks to* JANE AUSTEN.) And yet, it is not the style of a woman, no certainly, it is too strong and concise. No doubt he is a sensible man, and when he takes a pen in hand his thoughts naturally find proper words, it is so with some men. Yes, I understand that sort of mind. Vigorous, decided, not coarse. A better written letter than

I had expected. Still, a woman is not to marry a man merely because he can write a tolerable letter.

HARRIET. And it is but a short letter, too. And what shall I do?

She exits.

Scene 4

Enter MR KNIGHTLEY *in high spirits.*

MR KNIGHTLEY. I have good reason to believe that your little friend Harriet will soon hear of something to her advantage.

EMMA. Indeed? Of what sort?

MR KNIGHTLEY. A very serious sort, I can assure you.

EMMA. Very serious. I can think of but one thing.

MR KNIGHTLEY. I have reason to think that Harriet Smith will soon have an offer of marriage, and from a most unexceptionable quarter. Robert Martin is the man. He is desperately in love and means to marry her. I never hear better sense from anyone than Robert Martin. He is open, straightforward, and very well judging. I had no hesitation in advising him to marry.

EMMA. And Harriet had no hesitation in refusing.

General shock on stage.

NIECES. Refusing?!

MR KNIGHTLEY. Then she is a greater simpleton than I ever believed her. What is the foolish girl about?

EMMA. Oh, to be sure, it is always incomprehensible to a man that a woman should ever refuse an offer of marriage. A man always imagines a woman to be ready for anybody who asks her.

MR KNIGHTLEY. So, this is your doing. You persuaded her to refuse him. Emma, you have been no friend to Harriet Smith.

EMMA. She is superior to Mr Robert Martin. There can
scarcely be any doubt that her father is a gentleman, and a
gentleman of fortune. She may well make a superior match.
I believe Mr Elton has shown considerable interest.

MR KNIGHTLEY. Mr Elton? Pshaw! Ludicrous! I perceive
that your intimacy with Harriet will be a very unfortunate
one for her. You will puff her up with such ideas of her own
beauty that within a little while, nobody within her reach
will be good enough for her. Vanity working on a weak
head produces every sort of mischief. Miss Harriet Smith
may not find offers of marriage flow in so fast, though she
is a very pretty girl. Men of sense, whatever you may
choose to say, do not want silly wives. Let her marry Robert
Martin and she is safe, respectable and happy forever. But if
you encourage her to expect to marry greatly, she may be a
parlour boarder at Miss Goddard's all the rest of her life, or
till she grows desperate and is glad to catch at the old
writing master's son.

MR KNIGHTLEY *walks off in disgust.*

EMMA (*shouts after Knightley*). I do not always feel so
absolutely satisfied with myself, so entirely convinced that
my opinions are right as you, Mr Knightley.

ALL NIECES. Yeah, Mr Knightley, Rightley etc.,

Scene 5

HARRIET. Oh what a lovely house, Mr Elton's house, Such a
sweet beautiful house, and such beautiful yellow curtains.
(*Etc.*)

EMMA (*to* JANE AUSTEN). It is a very vulgar house.

JANE AUSTEN. Yes, but she is in love.

EMMA. True. Could you contrive of some way of us going in?

JANE AUSTEN. Later, perhaps.

HARRIET. I do so wonder Miss Woodhouse, that you should
not be married, or going to be married, so charming as you
are.

EMMA. My being charming Harriet, is not quite enough to induce me to marry. I must find other people charming – one other person at least. But I have very little intention of ever marrying. I believe few married women are half as much mistress of their husband's house, as I am of Hartfield.

HARRIET. But then to be an old maid at the last, like Miss Bates.

NIECE TWO. Who is Miss Bates?

JANE AUSTEN. An impoverished acquaintance, who despite her professed charity, Emma generally neglects to visit.

Arch look from EMMA.

NIECE THREE. I don't want to be her.

HARRIET. Do you know Miss Bates's niece?

NIECE ONE. Who is Miss Bates's niece?

JANE AUSTEN. Jane Fairfax. A beautiful and elegant young woman . . .

NIECE THREE. I want to be her!

JANE AUSTEN. . . . learned and accomplished in many fields, particularly that of music. Her piano playing is a delight.

EMMA. I'll practise, I'll practise. Tomorrow for at least an hour.

HARRIET. Practise what?

EMMA. My piano playing.

HARRIET. Oh, but you play so beautifully.

JANE AUSTEN. As I was saying, Jane Fairfax, though so full of accomplishments, is but poorly situated and will very likely end her days as a governess.

NIECE TWO *gains part.* EMMA *eyes her as she is speaking.*

EMMA. Oh we are always forced to be acquainted every time she comes to Highbury. Heaven forbid that I should ever bore people half so much about all the Knightleys together as Miss Bates does about Jane Fairfax. Every letter from her is read forty times over, her compliments to all friends go round and round again and if she does but knit a pair of garters for her grandmother, one hears of nothing else for a month. One is sick of the very name of Jane Fairfax! (NIECE ONE *comes forward to protect* NIECE TWO *from this character assassination and is caught up as* MISS BATES.) Why, Miss Bates, have you heard from Miss Fairfax recently? I hope she is well.

MISS BATES. Thank you, So kind and obliging, please do come in and visit. (NIECE THREE *slams down a letter*.) Oh, there it is, I was sure it could not be far off, but I had put my huswife upon it you see, without being aware, and so it was quite hid, but I had had it in my hand so very lately, that I was sure it must be upon the table. I was reading it to Mrs Cole. Have you received your invitation to the Coles?

HARRIET. Oh, yes, yes!

EMMA. No, I am not expecting one. (*Aside to the audience.*) A rather inferior family.

MISS BATES. I was reading it again to my mother, for it is such a pleasure to her, a letter from Jane – and she can never hear it often enough, so I knew it could not be far off and there it was, only just under my huswife and since you are so kind to wish to hear what she says – but first of all, I really must in justice to Jane, apologise for her writing so short a letter, only two pages you see, hardly two, and in general she fills the whole paper and crosses half. My mother often wonders that I can make it out so well. And indeed though my mother's eyes are not so good as they were, she can see amazingly well still, thank God, with the help of spectacles. But Jane is coming to us soon and she is to have three months with us at least.

EMMA. Oh, what a very great pleasure.

MISS BATES. Jane caught a cold, poor thing, so long as the seventh of November – as I am going to read to you – and has never been well since. A long time is it not, for a cold to hang upon her. She never mentioned it before because she would not alarm us. Just like her. So considerate. But however, she is so far from well that her friends, the Campbells, think she had better come home and try an air that always agrees with her, and nobody could nurse her as we do.

EMMA. I'm afraid I must be running away.

MISS BATES. The letter!

HARRIET *and* EMMA *carry on their journey.*

Scene 6

EMMA. I have a charitable visit to pay to a poor sick family.

NIECES *lie down as sick family whilst* EMMA *dispenses medicine.*

NIECE TWO. Emma was very compassionate, and the distresses of the poor were as sure of relief from her kindness, as her purse. She understood their ways, could allow for their ignorance, had no romantic expectations of extraordinary virtue from those whom education had done so little, entered into their troubles with ready sympathy, and always gave her assistance with as much intelligence as good will.

EMMA. These are the sights, Harriet, to do one good. How trifling they make everything else appear. I feel now as if I could think of nothing else but these poor creatures all the rest of the day.

HARRIET. Very true, poor creatures, one can think of nothing else.

EMMA. And really, I do not think the impression will soon be over.

HARRIET. Oh dear, no.

MR ELTON *appears. He could have spotted them when they walked past his house earlier and commented on the yellow curtains and he could have followed them surreptitiously to here.*

EMMA. On the other hand, we have done all we can. (*She walks over the bodies.*) Mr Elton!

MR ELTON. My dear ladies! What an unexpected surprise! May I have the honour of accompanying you?

EMMA (*aside to audience*). How fortunate to meet on a charitable visit. This should bring about an increase of love on both sides. Surely a good time for him to propose, were I anywhere but here. (*To* MR ELTON *and* HARRIET.) Please walk on while I attend to my lace.

EMMA *bends over.* MR ELTON *gives her a lustful look before walking on with* HARRIET. EMMA *tries to keep her distance but keeps catching up.* MR ELTON *talks about food. They reach the vicarage.*

MR ELTON. Oh, you must excuse me. I have a sermon to attend to . . .

EMMA *looks at* JANE AUSTEN *who points at* EMMA*'s lace.* EMMA *rips it off.*

EMMA. Part of my lace is gone and I do not know how I am to contrive, Mr Elton, I must beg leave to stop at your house and ask your housekeeper for a bit of ribbon or string.

MR ELTON. Certainly. (*Calling.*) Nelly!!

The housekeeper NELLY *enters and engages* EMMA *in conversation.*

NELLY. I hear the political situation in France is still very troublesome. Do you think the economic crisis will reach Britain, Miss?

EMMA. Mmm. Yes . . . Quite so . . . very good bilberry jam, Nelly.

NELLY. What do you think of the new poetry, Miss?

EMMA. Milk and two sugars – yes, shocking rain isn't it . . .

EMMA *enters* ELTON*'s room.*

MR ELTON. Ah, Miss Woodhouse! We were just talking of . . .

EMMA. Yes?

HARRIET. A wonderful Camembert that he tasted last night.

EMMA. How delightful! (*Aside to audience.*) Cautious, very cautious. He advances himself, inch by inch and will hazard nothing until he believes himself secure. He must now be left to himself. There are people who, the more you do for them, the less they will do for themselves.

Scene 7

EMMA *and the nieces play together.* EMMA *is aware that* MR KNIGHTLEY *has come into the room and is watching her.*

EMMA. What a comfort it is that we think alike about our nephews and nieces. As to men and women, our opinions are sometimes very different, but with regard to these children, we never disagree.

MR KNIGHTLEY. If you were as little under the power of fancy and whim in your dealings with men as you are where these children are concerned, we might always think alike.

EMMA. To be sure, our discordances must always rise from my being in the wrong.

MR KNIGHTLEY. Yes, and reason good. I was sixteen years old when you were born.

EMMA. And no doubt you were much my superior in judgement at that period of our lives; but does not the lapse of one and twenty years bring our understandings a good deal nearer?

MR KNIGHTLEY. Yes – a good deal nearer.

EMMA. But still not near enough to give me a chance of being right.

MR KNIGHTLEY. I have still the advantage of you by sixteen-years experience, and by not being a pretty young woman and a spoilt child. Come, my dear Emma, let us be friends and say no more about it. (*To a* NIECE.) Tell your aunt, little Emma, that she ought to set you a better example than to be renewing old grievances and that if she were not wrong before, she is now.

EMMA. That is true, very true. Little Emma, grow up a better woman than your Aunt. Be infinitely cleverer and not half so conceited.

Scene 8

NIECES (*chanting*).
Elton Harriet / Kiss it Marry it.
Elton Harriet / Kiss it Marry it.
Elton Harriet / Kiss it Marry it.
Elton Harriet / Kiss it Marry it.

NIECES *drift away and* HARRIET *turns to* EMMA.

HARRIET. Oh Miss Woodhouse, do you really think you should have asked Mr Elton to contribute to my book of riddles?

EMMA. Certainly Harriet. What better means could there be of allowing him to declare his feelings for you.

MR ELTON *appears, clutching a piece of paper.*

MR ELTON. Good day ladies. I have a charade for Miss Smith's excellent book. (*To* EMMA.) Miss Woodhouse, you are to be highly commended in furthering the young lady's education in this manner. It was written by . . . by a friend . . . to a young lady who was the object of his admiration. Perhaps you may not dislike looking at it.

He hands the riddle to EMMA. *She passes it to* HARRIET. MR ELTON *leaves and* HARRIET *reads the riddle. The nieces are curious about what it says.*

HARRIET.
My First Displays the Wealth and Pomp of Kings.
Lords of the Earth! Their Luxury and Ease.
Another View of Man, My Second Brings,
Behold Him There, The Monarch of the Seas!
Thy Ready Wit the Word Will Soon Supply.
May Its Approval Beam in That Soft Eye.

What can it be Miss Woodhouse? I have not an idea. I never saw anything so hard. What can it possibly be? 'Behold him there, the monarch of the seas' . . . Is it Neptune? . . . Or a mermaid? Or a shark?

NIECE ONE. Shark's only got one syllable.

NIECE TWO. Octopus.

NIECE THREE. Dolphin.

HARRIET. Does Mr Elton think I am like a dolphin? Would that be a favourable sign Miss Woodhouse?

EMMA. Dolphins and Sharks! Nonsense my dear Harriet. (EMMA *takes the paper and reads.*) 'My first displays the wealth and pomp of kings' That is 'COURT'. 'Behold him there, the monarch of the seas'. That is . . . (*She tries to encourage* HARRIET *to guess.*)

HARRIET (*thinking deeply*). BOAT!! Court boat . . . ??

EMMA. 'SHIP' Court Ship.

HARRIET (*smiling confidently*). Court Ship?!

EMMA. Courtship, Harriet, Courtship. (NIECES *cheer.*) Read it in comfort to yourself. There can be no doubt of it being written for you.

HARRIET. For me! From Mr Elton! Who might marry anybody! It is so much beyond anything I deserve. I do think it is the best riddle I have ever read. It is longer than any we have had before.

EMMA. Length is not everything Harriet. But a poet in love must be encouraged. Why don't you write it down in your book?

HARRIET *wanders off.*

EMMA (*chanting, and* NIECES *joining discreetly*).
Elton Harriet / Kiss it Marry it.
Elton Harriet / Kiss it Marry it.

Merging into:

Ding Dong Merrily On High . . . etc . . .

EMMA *departs.*

Scene 9

NIECES. Christmas Eve!

NIECE FOUR. Dinner at the Westons!

NIECE TWO. But Harriet has a bad cold.

NIECES *dance in a circle chanting.*

NIECES(*chanting*). Poor little Harriet. She's got a cold. Stay at home and do what you're told.

NIECES *make the sound of horses pulling* EMMA *and* MR KNIGHTLEY *in carriage.*

EMMA. Well, it appears Mr Knightley, that you are somewhat in error regarding Mr Elton's affections for Harriet. The way he rode all the way to London to have my portrait of her framed seems to indicate a great deal of affection.

MR KNIGHTLEY. For her or for you?

EMMA. Pshaw! Affection for me? What an idea! Harriet is terribly sick with a sore throat and Mr Elton will surely visit her. I very much doubt that we will be seeing him tonight.

Arrival – nieces neigh and stop trotting noises. Door is opened by a spruce MR ELTON.

EMMA. Why, Mr Elton!

MR ELTON. Miss Woodhouse.

EMMA. How nice to see you.

The party, with MR ELTON *getting drunk. The party guests stay static and chatting. The conversation turns to* FRANK CHURCHILL.

MR ELTON. Ah, Mrs Weston! How goes the sacred union of marriage? And when are we to expect your stepson, the dashing Frank Churchill?

MRS WESTON. He has been wanting to come to us ever since September. Every letter has been full of it, but he cannot command his own time. But now I have no doubt of seeing him in the second week of January.

MISS BATES *crosses stage, speaking.*

MISS BATES. Frank Churchill should be among us soon. He wrote to his new mother on the occasion of her marriage. I suppose you've heard of the handsome letter Mr Frank Churchill has written to Mrs Weston? I understand it was a very handsome letter indeed. Mr Woodhouse saw the letter and he says he never saw such a handsome letter in his life.

MR WOODHOUSE. Yes, it was an exceedingly good, pretty letter – written from Weymouth and dated twenty-eighth of September, and began: 'My dear Madam', but I forget how it went on, and it was signed Frank Weston Churchill.

JANE AUSTEN. There was something in the name, in the idea of Mr Frank Churchill, which always interested Emma. She had frequently thought – especially since his father's marriage to Miss Taylor – that if she were to marry, he was the very person to suit her.

EMMA. He ought to come, if he could stay only a couple of days – and one can hardly conceive a young man's not having it in his power to do as much as that.

MR WOODHOUSE. Snow! Snow!

NIECES *run to the window and stretch their arms out.*

NIECES (*almost singing*). Snowwww Snowwww.

General flurry of guests leaving.

MR KNIGHTLEY. Your father will not be easy, why do not you go?

EMMA. I am ready if the others are.

MR KNIGHTLEY. Shall I ring the bell?

EMMA. Yes, do.

NIECES (*singing*). I saw three ships come sailing in . . . (*Etc.*)

MR ELTON *gets into* EMMA's *carriage to the sound of trotting again. Silence from them, then Elton grabs her.*

MR ELTON. Oh Miss Woodhouse, Oh this ardent attachment, this unequal love, this . . . fearing, this hoping . . . I am ready to die. You Emma, only you . . .

EMMA. I am very much astonished, Mr Elton, this to me – you forget yourself – you mistake me for my friend – any message to Miss Smith I should be happy to deliver, but no more of this to me if you please.

MR ELTON. Miss Smith? A message to Miss Smith? What can you possible mean?

EMMA. Mr Elton, this is the most extraordinary conduct and I can account for it in only one way; you are not yourself. Command yourself enough to say no more and I will endeavour to forget it.

Trotting stops.

MR ELTON. Oh this uncontrollable desire, this unparalleled passion, this tumescent . . .

EMMA. It is impossible for me to doubt any longer. You have made yourself too clear. After such behaviour as I have witnessed during the past month to Miss Smith, to be addressing me in this manner – this is an unsteadiness of character which I had not supposed possible. Believe me sir, I am far, very far from gratified in being the object of such professions.

MR ELTON. Good heavens, what can be the meaning of this. Miss Smith? I never thought of Miss Smith in the whole course of my existence – never paid her any attentions but as your friend – never cared if she were dead or alive but as your friend. Oh, Miss Woodhouse, who can think of Miss Smith when Miss Woodhouse is near? Everything I have done for many weeks past has been with the sole view of marking the adoration of yourself. You cannot really, seriously, doubt it. No, I am sure you have seen and understood me. Charming Miss Woodhouse, let me interpret this interesting silence. It confesses that you have long understood me.

EMMA. No, Sir, it confesses no such thing. I have been in a most complete error with respect to your views till this moment. Am I to believe that you have never sought to recommend yourself particularly to Miss Smith?

MR ELTON. Never, Madam, never I assure you. I wish her extremely well; and no doubt there are men who might not object to – everybody has their level; but as for myself, I need not so totally despair of an equal alliance. No, madam, my visits to Hartfield have been for yourself only, and the encouragement I received.

Trotting starts again.

EMMA. Encouragement – I gave you encouragement? Sir, you
have been entirely mistaken in supposing it. It is as well the
mistake ends as it does. Had the same behaviour continued,
Miss Smith might have been led to a misconception of your
view, not being aware any more than myself, of the very
great inequality, which you are so sensible of. As to me, I
have no thought of matrimony at present.

NIECES *stop trotting and neigh! They break away and sit
down as* EMMA *exits the carriage.*

NIECES (*singing*).
Boyfriend, boyfriend, yes I had your boyfriend.

Scene 10

EMMA *arrives home.*

MR WOODHOUSE. A bowl of gruel, my dear?

EMMA. No thank you Papa, it's time for bed.

MR WOODHOUSE. Goodnight my dear.

*In a state of deep mortification she kisses him goodnight
and he leaves. Finally she and* JANE AUSTEN *are alone in
the bedroom.*

JANE AUSTEN. The hair was curled and the maid sent away,
and Emma sat down to think and be miserable. It was a
wretched business indeed. Such an overthrow of everything
she had been wishing for, such a development of everything
most unwelcome. Such a blow for Harriet. That was the
worst of all. Every part of it brought pain and humiliation
of some sort or other, but Emma's suffering was small in
comparison to the pain that would be Harriet's.

EMMA. If I had not persuaded Harriet into liking the man,
I could have borne anything. He might have doubled his
presumption to me, but poor Harriet. She might never have
thought of him but for me. Oh, that I have been satisfied in
persuading her not to marry young Martin. There, I was
quite right, but there I should have stopped and left the
rest to time and chance. I was introducing her into good

company and giving her the opportunity of pleasing someone worth having, I ought not to have attempted more. I have been but half a friend to her. I am sure I have not an idea of anybody else who would be at all desirable for her . . . William Cox? Oh no, I could not endure William Cox – a pert young lawyer.

EMMA *falls asleep against* JANE AUSTEN *to be woken by* HARRIET.

Scene 11

HARRIET *walks happily across stage.*

HARRIET. Oh, what a lovely house! Mr Elton's house. Such a sweet, beautiful house! 'May its approval beam in that soft eye.'

EMMA (*to audience*). I can keep her in the dark no longer. I must tell her. (*To* JANE AUSTEN.) Would you care to break the news?

JANE AUSTEN *shakes her head.* EMMA *approaches* HARRIET *who looks expectantly at her.* EMMA *shakes her head.* HARRIET *immediately begins to bawl and cry.*

EMMA (*to audience*). She's taking it rather well. Oh, Harriet, I'm sorry.

HARRIET. Oh, Emma, you must not blame yourself. Mr Elton is so completely superior to me that I should never have aspired to win his heart. I do not deserve such a man.

EMMA. Perhaps he was rather . . .

HARRIET. Perfect, yes, I know, but . . . (*Starts to cry.*)

EMMA *looks chastened.*

EMMA. Oh dear. She is more resolutely in love than I knew. And is she not truly simple and artless? Surely it would profit me to be more like her.

JANE AUSTEN (*laughs heartily*). It is a bit late in the day for you to become simple and artless, Emma.

HARRIET. Oh! Mr Knightley is here. I cannot face anyone just now . . .

Hurries off.

EMMA. Mr Knightley.

MR KNIGHTLEY. Emma.

They are interrupted by the arrival of MRS WESTON *who walks gloomily across the stage.*

MRS WESTON. Emma Emma, Frank has been delayed again. He shall not now be with us next week as we had hoped.

NIECE FOUR. Who's Frank?

NIECE ONE. He's the handsome hero, Frank Churchill.

NIECE FOUR. Who's that?

NIECE ONE. Mr Weston's son, silly.

NIECE TWO. Why isn't he called Frank Weston then?

NIECE ONE. The Churchills adopted him after Mr Weston's first wife died.

NIECE FOUR. The Churchills. Are they wicked step-parents?

MRS WESTON. Mrs Churchill is so possessive; she seems to have a peculiar hold over Frank.

Exit MRS WESTON.

MR KNIGHTLEY. Yet another delay, Emma. The dashing Frank Churchill seems disinclined to visit Highbury.

EMMA. What nonsense. He wishes exceedingly to come; but the Churchills will not spare him.

MR KNIGHTLEY. If Frank Churchill had wanted to see his father, he would have contrived it. A man of three and twenty must be able to do so.

EMMA. It is very unfair to judge anyone's conduct without an intimate knowledge of their situation.

MR KNIGHTLEY. There is one thing, Emma, which a man can always do, and that is his duty. With vigour and resolution. A man must always . . .

MR WOODHOUSE. Emma, would it be safe to send a little pork to the Bates'?

EMMA. Of course, papa. (*To* KNIGHTLEY.) What were you saying?

MR KNIGHTLEY. A man must always . . .

MR WOODHOUSE. You think it will do them no harm?

EMMA. Of course not papa.

MR KNIGHTLEY. It is always possible for a man to . . .

MR WOODHOUSE. They must be sure not to fry it in grease. Do you not agree, Mr Knightley?

MR KNIGHTLEY. Yes.

EMMA. Anyway, I am sure that when he does arrive he will be a most agreeable young man, despite your being determined to think ill of him.

MR KNIGHTLEY. Not at all. I would be most ready to acknowledge his merits; but I hear of none, save that he is well grown and good looking.

EMMA. Well, let us be satisfied with that – at Highbury we do not often see good-looking young men.

MR KNIGHTLEY. Sounds rather like a young puppy to me.

Exit KNIGHTLEY, *passing* MISS BATES *entering.*

Scene 12

MISS BATES (*to* MR WOODHOUSE). A letter from Jane. (NIECES *spring up and chant 'letter from Jane' in unison throughout this speech.*) A letter from Jane, Mr Knightley, a letter from Jane. Jane Fairfax is coming to visit us. She sent us a letter, though it was not her usual time for doing so, I read it to my mother three times – her eyes are not so good as they were you know – excuse me, I must hurry off and make preparations. A letter from Jane. A letter from Jane. Ah Mr Woodhouse, a letter from Jane. Jane Fairfax is coming.

MR WOODHOUSE. What was that?

EMMA *and* NIECES (*shouting*). Jane Fairfax is coming!

   MISS BATES *exits passing* MR KNIGHTLEY *entering.*

MR KNIGHTLEY. Miss Fairfax is coming. Good. A most excellent young lady. Highly accomplished and refined. A marvellous piano player. And would you not agree Emma that she has that especially elegant sort of beauty, which you particularly admire?

EMMA. Yes.

NIECE FOUR. Who's Jane Fairfax? I've forgotten.

NIECE THREE. She's a famous actress who had an affair with the Prime Minister!

NIECE TWO. She's a pirate queen from the Amazon!

NIECE FOUR. She's the Empress of Russia!

NIECE ONE. Jane Fairfax grew up quietly, the only child of Mrs Bates' younger daughter until . . .

NIECE TWO. She ran away to sea and became a bloodthirsty buccaneer?

NIECE THREE. She killed three men in a duel and took to the hills with a band of resistance fighters?

NIECE FOUR. She chopped off their heads and . . .

NIECE ONE. Until her parents unfortunately died and she was adopted by the Campbell's. They are treating her well until she is old enough to take up a position as a governess.

NIECES TWO, THREE *and* FOUR (*disappointed*). Oh.

MR KNIGHTLEY. A woman of great distinction and merit.

   He exits. Pause.

NIECE THREE. Why don't you like her, Miss Woodhouse?

EMMA. Because she's too bloody perfect!

   She crosses back to centre. Enter MISS BATES *and* JANE FAIRFAX.

EMMA. Hello!

MISS BATES (*bursting with enthusiasm*). Have you heard the news? I heard it just now from Mrs Cole – have you received your invitation to their dinner party? No? I'm sure it must be on its way, such excellent people, the Coles, such charming neighbours – I must tell you my news – but I've forgotten to introduce Jane – of course you know her already – she's been reading Proust to Mama – a little over my head at times, but Mama seems to enjoy it. (MR KNIGHTLEY *enters.*) Oh look! There's Mr Woodhouse – we must say hello to him. Hello Mr Woodhouse.

MR KNIGHTLEY. Emma, I have some news that may interest you.

MISS BATES. Have you heard the news? Mr Elton is going to be married!

MR KNIGHTLEY. That was my news.

MISS BATES. I suppose there was never a piece of news more generally interesting. Come on Jane.

MISS BATES *wanders round stage, talking happily.*

MR WOODHOUSE (*collaring* MR KNIGHTLEY). Do you really think it would be safe to send some pork to Miss Bates? Our Hartfield pork is not like any other pork. It is quite safe, I assure you, so long as it is well boiled.

EMMA. Papa, Mr Elton is to be married.

MR WOODHOUSE. Married? But he was such a nice young man.

NIECE FOUR. I want to know about the handsome hero. Where's Frank Churchill?

MR WOODHOUSE. Mr Elton seemed to me very well off as he was. I do not understand his hurry to get married.

JANE AUSTEN *shushes her niece.* EMMA *leads* JANE FAIRFAX *round the stage.*

EMMA. You were at Weymouth at the same time as Frank Churchill, I believe? How is he? Is he a handsome young man?

JANE FAIRFAX. I believe he is generally thought so.

MR WOODHOUSE *is leading* MR KNIGHTLEY *round the stage.*

EMMA. Are his manners good?

JANE FAIRFAX. I believe they are generally thought so.

She retreats to be with MISS BATES.

MR WOODHOUSE (*to* MR KNIGHTLEY). They must be sure not to roast the pork. Nothing is more injurious to the health. Oh Miss Fairfax!

MR KNIGHTLEY (*catching up with* EMMA). Emma! How do you think your friend Harriet Smith will take the news of Mr Elton's betrothal?

EMMA. Quite well, I imagine.

HARRIET *enters bawling and exits.*

MR KNIGHTLEY. Emma do you think we might . . .

HARRIET *interrupts* EMMA*'s conversation to* MR KNIGHTLEY.

HARRIET. Oh, Miss Woodhouse. What do you think has happened? I was sheltering from the rain in the haberdasher's shop, and who should come in, but . . . Robert Martin.

Wails and runs off stage.

MR KNIGHTLEY. Emma . . . do you think . . .

NIECE TWO (*as* PAGEBOY). Mrs Weston.

MRS WESTON *arrives, excited.*

MRS WESTON. I have wonderful news for everyone! Frank comes tomorrow. (*Remaining* NIECES *cheer and applaud.*) We'll see him tomorrow to a certainty. Mr Weston and I are so happy.

Exit MRS WESTON.

MR KNIGHTLEY (*to* EMMA). Well. Frank Churchill.

EMMA. Yes.

MR KNIGHTLEY. Emma . . . could we possibly . . .

HARRIET *arrives.*

HARRIET. Oh, excuse me, Miss Woodhouse. I just came to apologise for the scene I caused. I am quite myself again.

Enter MISS BATES.

MISS BATES. Miss Woodhouse! (*Noticing* HARRIET.) Oh, hello Harriet, have you received your invitation to Mr Elton's wedding yet?

HARRIET *bawls and rushes off stage.*

MR KNIGHTLEY. Your friendship seems to be doing her the world of good, Emma.

MISS BATES (*to* MR WOODHOUSE). I just came to thank you for the loin of pork, such kind neighbours, I swear no one ever had. If there is one thing my mother likes more than Proust, it's a good joint of roasted pork.

MR WOODHOUSE. She roasted the pork! She roasted the pork! She roasted the pork!

MR KNIGHTLEY. Excuse me, I have some business to attend to.

Exit MR KNIGHTLEY.

EMMA. I'm worn out.

EMMA *falls asleep. Pause. Excited whispering among nieces.* FRANK CHURCHILL *enters from audience and bows gracefully.* NIECES *ogle him.*

NIECES. Who's that?!

FRANK CHURCHILL. Do I have the honour of addressing Miss Woodhouse? I have heard you praised, Miss Woodhouse, but believe me; even extravagant praise could do you little justice. I am Frank Churchill . . . (NIECES *scream.*) . . . and I am honoured to make your acquaintance.

EMMA. I am honoured to meet you, Mr Churchill. Please, let me show you our grounds.

They link arms and leave. NIECES *swoon.*

Scene 13

JANE AUSTEN. The next morning brought Mr Frank
   Churchill again.

NIECE ONE. When is the handsome hero actually going to do
   something, Auntie Jane?

   JANE AUSTEN *quietens the niece. Enter* FRANK
   CHURCHILL, MRS WESTON *and* EMMA.

FRANK CHURCHILL. Ah, Highbury! That airy, cheerful,
   happy-looking Highbury. It will be my constant attraction.

NIECE TWO. Their first pause was at the Crown Inn, an
   inconsiderable house.

   NIECE ONE *interrupts and begins to supply information.*
   Marches confidently to the front and says.

NIECE ONE (*reciting like times table*). The Crown Inn! The
   Crown Inn had been built many years ago for a ballroom,
   but such brilliant days had long since passed away and now
   the highest purpose for which it was ever wanted was to
   accommodate a whist club established among the gentlemen
   and half gentlemen of the place.

FRANK CHURCHILL. What a damn shame its original
   purpose should have ceased. It is long and handsome
   enough. No! There should be balls here every fortnight
   throughout the winter!

NIECES (*applauding*). A Ball! A Ball!

JANE AUSTEN. He spoke like a young man very much bent
   on dancing.

   They walk on, FRANK CHURCHILL *still convincing the*
   other two it is a good idea. JANE FAIRFAX *sits at side of*
   stage reading. MRS WESTON *drifts off.*

EMMA. I believe you visited the Bates yesterday. And how do
   you think Miss Fairfax is looking?

FRANK CHURCHILL. Ill, very ill. That is, if a lady can be
   allowed to look ill. She is so pale; she gives the appearance
   of ill-health. A most deplorable want of complexion.

EMMA. Well, at least there is no disputing about taste. You do admire her, except for her complexion.

FRANK CHURCHILL. I cannot separate Miss Fairfax and her complexion.

EMMA. I have known her from a child. It is natural to suppose that we should be intimate, but we never were. Perhaps it was from that wickedness on my side, which was prone to take disgust towards a girl, so idolised and cried up as she always was. And then her reserve. I never could attach myself to one so completely reserved.

FRANK CHURCHILL. It is a most repulsive quality indeed. One cannot love a reserved person.

EMMA. I have no reason to think ill of her – not in the least – except such perpetual cautiousness of word and manner, it's apt to suggest suspicions of there being something to conceal.

FRANK CHURCHILL. I couldn't agree with you more.

EMMA. An illicit love affair?

FRANK CHURCHILL. God forbid!

NIECES *gather round* JANE FAIRFAX.

ALL NIECES (*reciting*).
Poor Jane Fairfax, cold as stone.
Hasn't got a mother, she hasn't got a home.
She's got a secret, but she's all alone.
Poor Jane Fairfax, cold as stone.

NIECE THREE. What is her secret? A married man perhaps?

NIECE ONE (*solemnly*). Emma. Frank's gone away to London.

EMMA. When?

NIECE ONE. This morning, at breakfast. Sent for his chaise and left.

EMMA. But why?

NIECE ONE. To have his hair cut.

Fits of giggles from NIECES. *Enter* MR KNIGHTLEY.

MR KNIGHTLEY. Just the trifling silly fellow I took him for. (*Arch look from* EMMA.) And now, Emma, to business.

May I ask you if you are gracing us with your presence at the Coles' dinner party?

EMMA. You know perfectly well, I couldn't possibly.

MR KNIGHTLEY. A very great shame. (*Exits.*)

Scene 14

COLES' *dinner party. Hubbub around* EMMA *who becomes increasingly agitated.*

NIECE ONE / SERVANT WITH FLOWERS. Delivery for the Coles.

MRS COLE. Put them there. Carefully!

HARRIET. The blue dress with the white ribbon, or the yellow muslin with the blue ribbon, or the red crêpe and yellow muslin, or . . .

JANE FAIRFAX. I would really rather stay in and read.

MISS BATES. Oh no, my dear, you must come. The Coles are very respectable, but do be sure to wrap up. You are so fragile.

JANE AUSTEN *narrates as bustle continues.*

MRS WESTON. I shall be but one moment Mr Weston.

JANE AUSTEN. The Coles were a very good sort of people, friendly, liberal and unpretending, but on the other hand, they were of low origin, in trade, and only moderately genteel. Fortune had smiled upon them. They added to their house and their number of servants.

NIECES *turn into obedient servants. Look to* MRS COLE.

MRS COLE. Nelly, Perkins, thingamajig – I hope you scrub your hands before dinner. (*All* NIECES *lift hands to show.*) They are a disgrace, and these fish knives are quite unpresentable.

JANE AUSTEN. And they invited all to their large dining room. (*Guests and host sigh a greeting as they meet 'AHHHH'.*) They were very respectable in their way.

EMMA. But they ought to be taught that it is not for them to arrange the terms on which the superior families would visit them. Nothing should tempt me to go.

JANE AUSTEN. All received invitations except for her father and herself.

MRS WESTON. I suppose they know you do not dine out.

JANE AUSTEN. Emma felt, however, that she should like to have the power of refusal.

NIECE TWO. Invitation to the Coles.

EMMA takes the invitation.

JANE AUSTEN. And she was persuaded. (*Guests and host sigh in satisfaction 'Ahhhh.'*)

JANE AUSTEN, transforming into MR KNIGHTLEY, takes EMMA's arm to walk into the Coles' dinner party.

MRS COLE. Ah Miss Woodhouse! Mr Knightley! Welcome to my humble abode.

All party guests chatting.

NIECE THREE. A large square pianoforte had arrived at the Bates' for Miss Fairfax.

MISS BATES. Absolutely astonished – have no idea who could have sent it . . . *etc.*

EMMA. The illicit passion!

MRS COLE. I declare I do not know when I have heard anything that has given me more satisfaction! It always has quite hurt me that Jane Fairfax, who plays so delightfully, should not have an instrument.

SERVANT (*offstage*). Dinner is served!

Hubbub of guests as MRS COLE finds the right positions at dinner table.

ALL. Soup! (*All drink soup.*) Meat! (*All eat.*) Claret! (*All drink.*)

MRS WESTON (*to EMMA*). I have made a match between Mr Knightley and Jane Fairfax. What do you say to it?

EMMA. Mr Knightley and Jane Fairfax? How can you think of such a thing? Mr Knightley must not marry. I am amazed you should think it. Do not take on to matchmaking for you do it very ill. Jane Fairfax, Mistress of the Abbey? Oh no, no, no, no! Every feeling revolts. How would he bear having Miss Bates belonging to him?! Thanking him all day long for his (*Mimicking* MISS BATES.) 'great kindness in marrying Jane, so very kind and obliging!'.

MRS WESTON. Shame, Emma! Do not mimic her.

MISS BATES (*to* MRS COLE). So very kind and obliging. Such a delightful collation.

MRS COLE. Oh, it's nothing, just something I threw together. Perkins! We'll have music in the Orangery. Miss Woodhouse, would you like to kick us off with something?

EMMA. Miss Fairfax, after you.

JANE FAIRFAX. Miss Woodhouse, after you.

EMMA. No really, after you.

JANE FAIRFAX. No, after you.

EMMA. I insist!

JANE FAIRFAX *relents and goes to piano.*

MRS COLE (*claps and ad-libs to arrange the guests again*). Come on Mr Knightley, Miss Smith . . . etc.

JANE FAIRFAX *sits – nieces arrange themselves to listen. She sings a sweet Italian song. Her singing is beautiful. Applause.*

Next, EMMA *begins to sing something even more impressive – Puccini's 'O Mio Babbino Caro'.*

FRANK CHURCHILL *enters to listen.*

MRS COLE. Over here Mr Churchill, Miss Woodhouse is going to entertain us on the FortePiano.

EMMA*'s singing is not as successful as* JANE FAIRFAX*'s. She starts off well but falters horribly on the high notes. There is stunned silence, followed by applause.*

JANE AUSTEN. Emma did not repent her condescension in going to the Coles'.

EMMA. I must have delighted them. Oh, worthy people who deserve to be made happy!

JANE AUSTEN. There was, however, one circumstance of regret for Emma, relating to Jane Fairfax. She did unfeignedly and unequivocally regret the inferiority of her own piano playing and singing and she sat down and practised vigorously for an hour and a half.

Enter HARRIET *to find* EMMA *singing scales and playing the piano badly.*

HARRIET. Oh, if I could but play as well as you and Miss Fairfax.

EMMA. Don't class us together, Harriet. My playing is no more like hers than a lamp is to sunshine.

HARRIET. Well, I hate Italian singing. There's no understanding a word of it.

They both begin playing 'chopsticks' together.

Scene 15

EMMA *and* HARRIET *are taking a walk.*

NIECE ONE. Emma and Harriet are heading for the haberdasher's. Isn't that where Harriet ran into Robert Martin?

NIECE TWO. The handsome young farmer?

JANE AUSTEN. He is not really all that handsome . . . (*To herself.*) virile, I imagine.

NIECES *look bored.*

NIECE THREE. What does virile mean, Auntie?

NIECE ONE (*getting interested*). It means kissing. Is there any kissing in this story?

NIECE THREE. I'll do it! Let me kiss someone, Auntie Jane!

JANE AUSTEN (*coldly*). Why don't you go and be a nice shopkeeper, dear?

The niece sent to be the shopkeeper offers HARRIET *a ribbon.*

NIECE THREE. Try this ribbon, Miss. Guaranteed to drive virile young farmers into a passionate frenzy. They'll be leaping off their hay carts to kiss you.

HARRIET *does not seem displeased at this suggestion but* JANE AUSTEN *strides across stage and drags the niece off by her ear.* EMMA *leads* HARRIET *out of the shop.*

EMMA. These days one detects a certain lack of propriety amongst the lower classes . . . imagine . . . kissing.

HARRIET. Virile.

MISS BATES *and* MRS WESTON *arrive.*

EMMA. Why, Miss Bates, how pleasant to see you . . . and do you have a few hours worth of interesting stories about the charming Miss Fairfax?

MISS BATES. Yes!

EMMA. Oh, good!

Scene 16

MISS BATES. Jane did not catch a cold last night!

EMMA. Really!

MISS BATES. But she did enjoy the baked apples that Mr Knightley sent us!

EMMA. No!

MISS BATES. But she was most concerned about my mother's spectacles . . . the rivet came out this morning; she could not put them on. I meant to take them over to be repaired first thing but something or other hindered me all the morning, first we thought the chimney wanted sweeping then Jane would not eat her breakfast – she makes such a shocking breakfast, you would be quite frightened if you saw how little she eats, though about the middle of the day she gets hungry, and there is nothing she likes so well as those baked apples and they are extremely wholesome . . . I have so often heard Mr Woodhouse recommend a baked apple . . . the apples themselves are the finest sort although I am quite shocked you know, I learned that Mr Knightley has sent us the last of his supply and now has not one left for himself. Mrs Hodges, his servant, was quite distressed about it, really it was too generous of him . . . Where was I?

MRS WESTON. Your mother's spectacles.

MISS BATES. Ah, yes . . . My mother's spectacles. You know, this morning . . .

MRS WESTON (*interrupting quickly*). A rivet came out . . . and Frank is fixing them at this very moment. Come, let us see how he is managing.

The party enters the Bates' house. When they draw back the curtains that represent the Bates' house, we find FRANK CHURCHILL *and* JANE FAIRFAX *slightly startled.* FRANK CHURCHILL *is fixing the spectacles and* JANE FAIRFAX *is looking at her new piano.*

MISS BATES. Have you not finished yet?

FRANK CHURCHILL. I have not been working uninterruptedly. I have been assisting Miss Fairfax in eh . . . in eh . . .

JANE FAIRFAX. In making my piano stand steadily. It was not quite firm.

FRANK CHURCHILL. Yes. In making the piano stand steadily. The floor is shockingly uneven.

JANE FAIRFAX. Shockingly uneven.

HARRIET. No it's not.

EMMA. Shhhhhhh!

FRANK CHURCHILL (*to* EMMA). It is a pleasure to see you at least ten minutes earlier than I calculated.

Silence.

MISS BATES. A baked apple, anyone?

FRANK CHURCHILL. Miss Woodhouse, let me find the best one for you.

MRS WESTON. Will you demonstrate your new piano for us, Miss Fairfax?

They mill around listening to the piano.

NIECE FOUR. Auntie Jane, was there something going on there before everyone arrived?

JANE AUSTEN. What makes you say that, my little angel?

NIECE FOUR. Her blouse is unbuttoned.

JANE FAIRFAX *does up her blouse mid song.*

JANE AUSTEN. A mere oversight in dressing, I imagine . . . shouldn't you be getting ready for bed, sweetheart?

FRANK CHURCHILL. Shouldn't you be getting ready for bed, sweetheart?

ALL. What?!

FRANK CHURCHILL (*flustered*). I mean . . . I mean . . . (*Looks appealingly at* JANE AUSTEN. JANE AUSTEN *writes hurriedly.*) I mean, shouldn't we be getting ready for a good night's sleep in bed before we put on our dance . . . ? (FRANK CHURCHILL *looks at* JANE AUSTEN *as if this was not a very good rescue by her. She shrugs as if it was the best she could do.*)

MRS WESTON. What dance?

ALL. Yes, what dance?

FRANK CHURCHILL (*totally at a loss*). The dance that . . . the dance that . . . (*Looks again to* JANE AUSTEN. NIECES *giggle.*)

NIECE FOUR. I like him.

JANE AUSTEN. The confusion was forgotten with the arrival of Mr Knightley.

JANE AUSTEN *steps on as* MR KNIGHTLEY.

MR KNIGHTLEY. How is Miss Fairfax, Miss Bates? I came particularly to enquire after her health.

MISS BATES. She is most well. She . . .

MR KNIGHTLEY. Good. I am going to Kingston. Can I do anything for you while I am there?

MISS BATES. Most kind and obliging, but no, I cannot think of anything . . . but please come in and visit. Miss Woodhouse is here.

MR KNIGHTLEY. Well, for five minutes perhaps.

MISS BATES. And Mrs Weston and Frank Churchill, too.

MR KNIGHTLEY. No, not now. I thank you, but I must get on to Kingston as fast as I can.

MISS BATES. But you must hear Jane's new piano.

MR KNIGHTLEY. No, I cannot. I will call another day. Farewell.

Exit MR KNIGHTLEY. EMMA *walks round the stage with* FRANK CHURCHILL.

FRANK CHURCHILL (*loudly to* EMMA). What felicity it is to hear a tune, which has made one happy. Was it not thoughtful of whoever sent the piano to send music as well? (*To* JANE FAIRFAX.) Miss Fairfax, what was the name of that man we were with at Weymouth . . . the one who was having some problems with his wife . . . the one you were so friendly with?

EMMA (*quietly*). Hush! You speak too plain. She mustn't understand you.

FRANK CHURCHILL. I hope she does . . . (*Loudly.*) It was obviously a gift straight from the heart.

EMMA. Really, I wish I had never taken up with the idea.

FRANK CHURCHILL. I am very glad you did.

MISS BATES. Such beautiful playing.

FRANK CHURCHILL. Now that I think about it, would it not be a famous good idea to organise a dance? Since dancing at the Coles, I have been longing for some more.

MISS BATES. Such generous neighbours, the Coles! Although it is many years since I have danced. I believe that people are sometimes kissed after dances . . . not that I could bring myself to approve of such things of course. Does not Jane play exquisitely well?

EMMA. Yes, she does. I believe that there is nothing in the world I would rather do than listen to Jane Fairfax play the piano.

Scene 17

Exit MISS BATES *and* MISS FAIRFAX. EMMA, FRANK CHURCHILL *and* MRS WESTON *appear, meeting* MR WOODHOUSE *in the Weston's house.*

FRANK CHURCHILL. It may be possible to do without dancing entirely.

EMMA. Instances have been known of young people passing many months without it, with no material injury . . .

FRANK CHURCHILL. . . . but when a beginning has been made . . .

EMMA. . . . it must be a very dull set that does not ask for more.

FRANK CHURCHILL. Surely, mother, this room is large enough for five couples?

MRS WESTON. Oh, yes, I am sure it is. But five couples are hardly worth while standing up for. We could not invite so few.

FRANK CHURCHILL. Invite ten couples then, and use both rooms. Might we not use both rooms and dance across the passage?

MR WOODHOUSE. Oh no! It would be the extreme of imprudence. I could not bear it for Emma – Emma is not strong – she could catch a dreadful cold. Do not talk of such a wild thing.

FRANK CHURCHILL. Of course . . . we must not endanger Emma's health. We will use only one room . . . surely ten couples may stand here very well.

MR WOODHOUSE. That young man is not quite the thing. He is forever opening doors and letting in draughts.

EMMA. It would be a sad crowd . . . it would be dreadful to be standing so close . . . nothing can be further from pleasure than a crowd in a little room.

FRANK CHURCHILL. Miss Woodhouse, you have the art of giving pictures in a few words. A crowd in a little room – exquisite, quite exquisite . . . But could not ten couples stand here very well?

MR KNIGHTLEY. Ten couples in here? Pshaw!

MR KNIGHTLEY *strides back to the table and resumes role of* JANE AUSTEN.

JANE AUSTEN. And that was the end of that scheme.

FRANK CHURCHILL. Er, one moment, if you please . . . Miss Woodhouse, your inclination for dancing has not been frightened away, I hope, by the terror of my mother's little rooms. May I hope for the honour of your hand for the first two dances of this projected ball, to be given, not at Randalls, but at the Crown Inn?

MR WOODHOUSE. The Crown Inn?

EMMA. What an admirable notion!

MR WOODHOUSE. Not the Crown Inn! A very bad plan . . . We shall catch our deaths of cold.

EMMA. You may secure my company for the first two dances, Mr Churchill. It is an admirable idea. I shall look forward to it very much.

FRANK CHURCHILL *kisses* EMMA*'s hand and bows to* JANE AUSTEN.

JANE AUSTEN. I admire your determination, Mr Churchill.

MR KNIGHTLEY. Idle young puppy!

EMMA *dances ecstatically to Jackson 5. (Song – 'ABC'). Preferably the dance should be done with a ribbon stick. After a few bars,* EMMA *falls exhausted onto the floor.*

EMMA. I think I must be in love. I certainly must. This sensation of listlessness, weariness, stupidity, everything dull and insipid about the home. I must be in love. I should be the oddest creature in the world if I were not . . . For a few weeks at least.

Scene 18

At EMMA*'s house.* EMMA *and* MR KNIGHTLEY.

EMMA. You do not look forward to the dance?

MR KNIGHTLEY. I have nothing to say against it, but other people cannot choose my pleasures for me.

JANE FAIRFAX. Oh, Miss Woodhouse, I hope nothing may happen to prevent the Ball. I do look forward to it with great pleasure.

MR KNIGHTLEY. You do?

She and MR KNIGHTLEY *walk off together.*

EMMA (*to audience, slightly suspiciously*). I do not believe he is attracted to her.

FRANK CHURCHILL (*rushing on*). My stepmother has fallen ill. I have only time to bid farewell to my friends here before I go . . . I have just taken my leave of Miss Fairfax. (*Pause.*) Miss Woodhouse . . . I think you can hardly be without suspicion.

EMMA (*to audience*). He is more in love with me than I supposed.

FRANK CHURCHILL (*pause*). My regard for Hartfield is most warm. Goodbye! (FRANK CHURCHILL *rushes off.*)

EMMA (*to audience*). He is indeed an exceedingly pleasing young man . . . but am I in love with him?

Interval.

Scene 18 (*continued*)

EMMA. Frank Churchill . . . am I in love with him? . . . I think not . . . well perhaps a little, but my happiness is not too deeply involved . . . I am very fond of him, but if he were to ask, I would refuse.

NIECES (*amazed*). Refuse?!

EMMA. They say everybody is in love once in their lives, so I may conclude that I have been let off easily . . . I hope he will not take it too hard that I do not love him . . . Possibly I could yet steer him towards happiness . . . ?

  HARRIET *arrives flustered.*

HARRIET. He will soon be among us again.

EMMA. Who?

HARRIET. Who? Mr Elton! . . . and his bride! Oooooh!

EMMA. Harriet . . . Did you not think that Mr Churchill was an exceedingly fine young man?

HARRIET. Yes, Miss Woodhouse. But how am I to bear Mr Elton returning with his bride?

EMMA. Mr Churchill is really a very eligible young man!

JANE AUSTEN. Fortunately Emma now knew the danger of dwelling on such speculations.

EMMA. But think how advantageous it would be to Harriet . . .

Scene 19

NIECE ONE *and* TWO. Miss Woodhouse and Miss Smith pay their respects to Mr and Mrs Elton.

  AUGUSTA ELTON *is found in her house, like a state figure with* MR ELTON *by her side.* EMMA *and* HARRIET *enter. They raise their arms as though drinking tea and freeze.*

JANE AUSTEN. How peculiarly unlucky poor Mr Elton was in being in the same room at once with the woman he had just married, the woman he had wanted to marry, and the woman he had been expected to marry.

EMMA and HARRIET *exit. The protocol is dropped and* MRS ELTON *claps hands for servants to clear the tea.*

MRS ELTON. Oh, do hurry up, you clumsy so and so.

MR and MRS ELTON *are in a clinch kissing whilst* EMMA *and* HARRIET *journey home in a carriage.*

HARRIET (*wistfully*). Oh, is she not very beautiful and charming?

EMMA. Yes, very nicely dressed. A remarkably elegant hat.

HARRIET. He is just as superior as ever. To know he has not thrown himself away is such a comfort. He called her –

MR ELTON. Augusta!

HARRIET. How delightful. (*She sobs.*)

NIECES ONE *and* TWO. Mrs Elton visits Hartfield.

The NIECES *dutifully and elegantly stand wincing at* MRS ELTON'*s language and acting out what* EMMA *would never show.*

MRS ELTON. Very like Maple Grove! My brother, Mr Suckling's seat. He would be very enchanted with this place. People who have extensive grounds themselves are always pleased with anything in the same style. They will visit us in the spring and we will explore a great deal. They will have their barouche landau, of course. Do you know Bath? The ideal place for you and your father. A line from me would bring you a host of acquaintance.

NIECE ONE. Uugghhh! To be indebted to her for an introduction. How insufferably vile.

MRS ELTON. My resources make me quite independent. The world I could give up – parties, balls, plays. Blessed with so many resources within myself the world is not necessary to me. Miss Woodhouse, you and I must establish a musical club and have regular weekly meetings. Would

it not be a good plan? (*Sings 'Would it not be a good plan'.*
MR WOODHOUSE *then* EMMA *respond by trying to sing
'yes'.*) Can you guess who I met at the Westons? Knightley!
Knightley himself. (*The* NIECES *stiffen.*) Quite the
gentleman, I must say. (*Freezes.*)

NIECE TWO. Knightley! She called him Knightley!

MR WOODHOUSE. Mmm . . . a very pretty sort of young
lady. Pretty, obliging and very well behaved. I ought to have
paid my respects before.

EMMA. I never expected you to approve the marriage.

MR WOODHOUSE. Politeness, Emma.

MRS ELTON. Jane Fairfax is absolutely charming. I quite rave
about Jane Fairfax and it is up to us to help her. 'Full many
a flower is born to blush unseen, and waste its fragrance on
the desert air.' A vast deal may be done by those who dare
to act and I daresay we shall sometimes find a seat for her
in a barouche landau in some of our exploring parties.

MRS ELTON *crosses to* JANE FAIRFAX.

EMMA (*to audience*). Poor Jane Fairfax! She may be dabbling
with a dubious man but the kindness and protection of Mrs
Elton is sore punishment. She must have some motive more
powerful than appears for remaining in Highbury. (MR
KNIGHTLEY *joins her.*) I know how highly you think of
Jane Fairfax.

MR KNIGHTLEY. Yes, anybody may know how highly I think
of her.

EMMA. The extent of your admiration may take you by
surprise some day.

MR KNIGHTLEY. Oh! Are you there? You have been settling
that I should marry Jane Fairfax.

EMMA. No, indeed! I have not the slightest wish for your
marrying Jane Fairfax or Jane Anybody.

MR KNIGHTLEY. Jane Fairfax is a charming young woman
but she has her fault; She has not the open temper that a
man could wish for in a wife.

Scene 20

Enter JANE FAIRFAX. *She gingerly takes off her shoes
and stockings and paddles in water, dancing to Piazzolla.
Gradually all members of the cast surround her and upbraid
her for being out in the rain.*

MR KNIGHTLEY. I hope you didn't venture far this morning,
Miss Fairfax, or I'm sure you must have been wet.

JANE FAIRFAX. I went only to the post office. It's my daily
errand. A walk before breakfast does me good.

MR KNIGHTLEY. Not a walk in the rain, I should imagine.

*All characters stick their oars in about the rain and the post
office, wagging their fingers and tutting.*

MR WOODHOUSE. I am very sorry to hear, Miss Fairfax, of
your being out this morning in the rain. Young ladies should
take care of themselves. Young ladies are delicate plants.

JANE FAIRFAX. I am very much obliged by your kind
solicitude about me.

MRS ELTON. What's this I hear? Going to the post office in
the rain? This must not be you sad girl, how could you do
such a thing? I must positively exert my authority.

MISS BATES. You must not run such terrible risks, liable as
you are to such severe colds.

MRS ELTON. We will not allow her to do such a thing again. I
shall speak to Mr E. One of our men shall enquire for your
letters and bring them to you every morning.

JANE FAIRFAX. You are extremely kind, but I cannot give up
my early walk. I must walk somewhere and the post office
is an object. The post office is a wonderful establishment!
So seldom that any negligence or blunder appears. So
seldom that a letter amongst the thousands that are
constantly passing around our kingdom is even carried
wrong, and not one in a million actually lost. If one thinks
of all it has to do, and all that it does so well, IT REALLY
IS ASTONISHING!

Last passage said with too much gusto and they all back off.

EMMA (*to audience*). Quite obvious. Corresponding with her lover. I could have made an enquiry or two – but I am determined not to utter a word to hurt Jane Fairfax's feelings . . . (*All cast look at her.*) I mean it.

Scene 21

JANE FAIRFAX *approaches* EMMA *but* MRS ELTON *grabs her arm to draw her away.*

MRS ELTON. Here is April come already! Have you heard of any governess' position likely to suit you?

JANE FAIRFAX. I have not made any enquiry.

MRS ELTON. But, my dear we cannot begin too early.

JANE FAIRFAX. I have no doubt of meeting with something that will do – there are offices in town, which deal in human flesh.

MRS ELTON *is slightly shocked by this.*

MRS ELTON. Oh, my dear, human flesh! You quite shock me; if you mean a fling in the slave trade I assure you that Mr E and I were always rather friends of the abolition.

JANE FAIRFAX. I was not thinking of the slave trade; governess trade, I assure you, was all that I had in view.

MRS ELTON. I know you. You would take up with anything, but I shall be a little more nice on your behalf . . . There goes another dear old beau of mine. I assure you, I like him excessively. I admire all that quaint, old-fashioned politeness. Modern ease often disgusts me. But this good old Woodhouse, I wish you could have heard his gallant speeches to me at dinner. I begin to think my Caro Sposo would be absolutely jealous. He took notice of my gown. How do you like it? I have quite a horror of finery but a bride, you know, must appear like a bride.

HARRIET *enters with a box and walks across stage.* MRS ELTON *sniggers and* HARRIET, *on verge of tears, exits.*

HARRIET. Miss Woodhouse!

EMMA. Yes, Harriet.

> HARRIET *goes to speak, hesitates, then leaves. Enter* MRS WESTON, *waving a letter.*

MRS WESTON. A letter from Frank. The Churchills are moving to London. Now Frank can be with us whenever he chooses. We must prepare for the ball.

NIECES. The Ball! The Ball!

JANE AUSTEN. The Weston's ball was to be a real thing. A very few tomorrows stood between the young people of Highbury and happiness.

ALL. Hooray!!

EMMA. I am concerned for Frank Churchill's feelings. He is undoubtedly in love with me. I wish I might be able to keep him from an absolute declaration . . . that would be so painful for him . . . and yet I cannot help anticipating something decisive.

> FRANK CHURCHILL *arrives.*

FRANK CHURCHILL. Miss Woodhouse . . .

EMMA. Mr Churchill . . .

NIECE FOUR. He's going to propose!

FRANK CHURCHILL. My spirits flutter to be back at Hartfield.

NIECE THREE. Go on! Do it!

FRANK CHURCHILL. I must be off. (*Exits.*)

EMMA (*turning and frowning at* NIECES). You frightened him away.

NIECE ONE. Perhaps he is less in love with you than you think.

EMMA. Perhaps he does not trust himself to be alone with me for long!

NIECE THREE. Perhaps he might sweep you up in his arms and cover you with passionate kisses?!

JANE AUSTEN. He is moving to Richmond, a mere nine miles away. He will have every opportunity to visit again, if he wishes.

NIECE TWO. Is he going to propose?

JANE AUSTEN. Wait and see.

NIECES. Aaaawww! . . .

Scene 22

NIECES *walk forward rather dejectedly. On reaching the front they become excited.*

NIECES. The Ball at the Crown Inn.

NIECES ONE *and* TWO. Miss Emma Woodhouse and Miss Harriet Smith.

FRANK CHURCHILL. I think Mrs Elton must be here soon. I have a great curiosity to see her – I have heard so much of her.

NIECES ONE *and* TWO. Mr and Mrs Elton.

FRANK CHURCHILL. But Miss Bates and Miss Fairfax! We thought you were to bring them.

All guests gasp and freeze.

JANE AUSTEN. The mistake had been slight. The carriage was sent for.

MRS ELTON. Well! What a fine young man Churchill is. I am extremely pleased with him. You may believe me, I never compliment – so truly the gentleman without the least conceit or puppyism. You must know I have a vast dislike to puppies – quite a horror of them.

NIECES ONE *and* TWO. Miss Jane Fairfax and Miss Hettie Bates.

MISS BATES. No rain at all! Nothing to signify. Well, this is brilliant indeed. My dear Mrs Elton, so kind and obliging, most comfortable carriage. My dear Jane, are you sure you did not wet your feet? Oh, Mr Frank Churchill – my mother's spectacles have never been in fault since. Such a noble fire, I am quite roasted.

MRS ELTON. Churchill! How do you like my gown? How do you like my trimming? How is my hair? Nobody can think less of dress than I do, but when everyone's eyes are so much upon me . . . the ball I have no doubt is chiefly in my honour, you know.

EMMA (*to* FRANK CHURCHILL). How do you like Mrs Elton?

FRANK CHURCHILL. Not at all. When are we to begin dancing?

JANE AUSTEN. Emma could hardly understand him; he seemed in such an odd humour. There was a restlessness, which showed a mind not at ease. What was worse was as a recent bride Mrs Elton must be asked to begin the ball. She would expect it. Emma bore the sad truth with fortitude. It was almost enough to make her think of marrying.

General applause. JANE AUSTEN *assumes the role of* MR KNIGHTLEY. *The dance is formed and sets off in a line like a Scottish reel to the music of 'The Reel of the 51st'.* EMMA *dances with* FRANK CHURCHILL. *She sees* MR KNIGHTLEY *and the dance freezes.*

NIECE TWO. Emma was more disturbed by Mr Knightley's not dancing than by anything else. He ought to be dancing, not classing himself with the husbands and fathers. His tall, firm, upright figure among the bulky forms and stooping shoulders of the elderly men, was such as Emma felt must draw everybody else's eyes – there was not one among the whole row of young men who could be compared to him.

The dance ends, all clap, all call for another. HARRIET *has no partner.*

MISS BATES. Why Mr Elton! Do you not dance?

MR ELTON. Most readily, if you will dance with me.

MISS BATES. Me! Oh no! Miss Smith has no partner.

MR ELTON. Miss Smith. Oh . . . I had not observed. (HARRIET *is right next to* MR ELTON.) Well. If I were not an old married man, but my dancing days are over.

HARRIET *fights back the tears as she sees smiles pass between* MR ELTON *and his wife. The dance is about to begin when* MR KNIGHTLEY *leads her to the dance floor.*

MRS ELTON. Knightley has taken pity on poor little Miss Smith – very good-natured, I declare.

Dance ends, dancers leave EMMA *and* MR KNIGHTLEY. *The* ELTONS *laugh unpleasantly.*

MR KNIGHTLEY. Why is it that they are your enemies?

EMMA. I wanted Harriet to marry him and they cannot forgive me.

MR KNIGHTLEY. I shall not scold you. I leave you to your own reflections.

EMMA. Can you trust me? With such flatterers? Does my vain spirit ever tell me I am wrong?

MR KNIGHTLEY. Not your vain spirit but your serious spirit. If one leads you wrong, I am sure the other tells you of it.

EMMA. I do own myself to have been completely mistaken in Mr Elton. There is a littleness about him, which you discovered and I did not.

NIECE ONE. The last dance. Come on everyone come on. (*Etc . . . random chatter.*)

EMMA. I am ready whenever I am wanted.

MR KNIGHTLEY. Whom are you going to dance with?

EMMA. With you, if you will ask me.

MR KNIGHTLEY. Will you?

EMMA. Indeed I will. We are really so much brother and sister as to make it not at all improper.

MR KNIGHTLEY. Brother and sister? No, indeed!

Dance peels away. NIECES *turn into gypsies singing folk tunes.*

Scene 23

HARRIET *and* MISS BICKERTON *walking in country picking flowers.*

HARRIET. Don't make a fuss, but isn't that a band of gypsies?

Three GYPSIES *stand up.* MISS BICKERTON *screams and runs off.*

GYPSY WOMAN. Help a poor family, miss. Buy this bunch of flowers – only a penny.

HARRIET. I cannot . . . I haven't . . . my purse is at . . . oh . . .

GYPSY WOMAN. Only a penny.

HARRIET. Get away! Get back!

HARRIET *tries to flee and trips melodramatically.*

GYPSY WOMAN. Don't just stand there Shaun – help the lady up.

HARRIET. Aaaaaaaaahhhhhhh!!!

She flees, crashing into FRANK CHURCHILL *and they exit together.*

GYPSY WOMAN. Inbred, I expect. Come along kids.

They exit. Enter EMMA.

EMMA. That was a considerably pleasurable evening. Harriet cured of her infatuation, Frank Churchill not too much in love with me and Mr Knightley not wishing to quarrel. How very happy a summer must lie before me.

FRANK CHURCHILL *enters carrying* HARRIET.

NIECE TWO. Frank Churchill with Harriet in his arms. Something extraordinary must have happened.

HARRIET *is placed into a chair. All fluster round and* EMMA *calls for smelling salts.*

HARRIET. I was walking out with Miss Bickerton beyond Highbury – when the road became deeply sheltered by elms and before us suddenly, there was a hoard of gypsies! A dirty child came forward and begged and Miss Bickerton screamed and ran up a steep bank expecting me to follow. But I suffered from a cramp from last night's dancing and I fell. And then they were upon me – a fat monster woman and her giant son and loads of others clamouring for money.

NIECES (*taking part of gypsies, waving sticks and shouting*). Money! Argent! Vive la Revolution! (*Singing.*) Allons enfants de la patrie, Le jour de gloire est arrive!

JANE AUSTEN. Such an adventure as this, a fine young man and a lovely young woman thrown together in such a way could hardly fail to suggest ideas to the coldest heart and the steadiest brain. Could a linguist, a grammarian, could even a mathematician have seen what Emma saw, without feeling that circumstances had been at work? Everything was to take its natural course, however, neither impelled nor assisted. She would not stir a step, nor drop a hint; she had had enough of interference.

MR WOODHOUSE *stands.*

MR WOODHOUSE. I have heard it all. It's known all over Highbury. You must promise, Emma, never to go beyond the shrubbery again.

EMMA. Yes, father.

FRANK CHURCHILL. And now I really must be getting back to Richmond.

NIECES *watch him leave.*

HARRIET. I have something I should like to tell you all. A sort of confession. And then it will all be over. I am now going to destroy what I ought to have destroyed long ago. Can not you guess what is inside this box?

EMMA. Did Mr Elton give you anything?

HARRIET (*reads label on box*). 'Most precious treasures'. (*She reverentially opens box.*)

EMMA. Sticking plaster?

HARRIET. Do you not remember him cutting his finger with your penknife and you recommending sticking plaster? I gave him some of mine and in my nonsense I made a treasure of what was left.

EMMA. I deserve to be under a continual blush all the rest of my life. I had plenty in my pocket all the while. Oh my sins – what else?

HARRIET. Here, here is something still more valuable, because this really did belong to him.

NIECE THREE. The end of an old pencil.

NIECE ONE. The part without any lead.

HARRIET. This was really his. He left it on the table when he had cut it nearly all away. I am going to throw them both on the fire and I wish you to see me do it.

EMMA. But Harriet, I've not a word for the bit of old pencil, but the sticking plaster might be useful.

HARRIET. No! I must burn them both now. (*She hurls them on to the fire.* NIECES *shriek in agony.*) An end, thank heaven, of Mr Elton!

EMMA (*to audience*). And when will there be a beginning of Mr Churchill?

JANE AUSTEN. Mr Knightley, having taken an early dislike to Frank Churchill was only growing to dislike him more. He began to suspect him of some double-dealing in his pursuit of Emma. He began to suspect him of some inclination to trifle with Jane Fairfax.

MR KNIGHTLEY. My dear Emma, do you think you perfectly understand the degree of acquaintance between the gentleman and the lady we have been speaking of?

EMMA. Between Mr Frank Churchill and Miss Fairfax. Oh yes, perfectly!

MR KNIGHTLEY. Have you ever at any time had any reason to think that he admired her or that she admired him?

EMMA. Never! Never! How did this possibly come into your head?

MR KNIGHTLEY. I have lately imagined that I saw symptoms of attachment between . . .

EMMA. Oh, you amuse me excessively! They are as far from an attachment to one another as any two human beings in the world can be. Vain imaginings, Mr Knightley – I believed you above them.

EMMA *waltzes off.*

Scene 24

TWO NIECES *at front of stage.*

NIECE ONE. I want something exciting to happen.

NIECE TWO. Me too.

NIECE THREE. And me.

NIECE TWO. I'm getting bored with all this tactical manoeuvring. If I was Emma, I'd punch Mrs Elton on the nose, lock Frank Churchill in a bedroom with Harriet, marry off Jane Fairfax to a passing millionaire and then go out and get me a man.

NIECES. Yeah!

JANE AUSTEN. In this state of schemes and hopes and connivance, June opened upon Hartfield.

MR KNIGHTLEY (*to* EMMA). I hope that you will soon visit me at Donwell Abbey . . . the strawberries are ripening fast.

MRS ELTON (*overhearing*). I accept! You may depend on me Knightley! Name the day and I'll bring friends.

Getting more involved in the plans.

I'll wear my large bonnet, and a nice little basket on my arm. (*Ad lib . . . there can be donkeys etc . . .*)

NIECE TWO. Strawberry picking expedition to Donwell Abbey.

NIECES. Strawberries!

All cast move to the front of the stage to pick strawberries, except MR ELTON *who observes them from behind.*

MRS ELTON. Strawberries – the best fruit in England – always wholesome, the finest sorts here, best time in the morning, never get tired collecting them. Hautboys are the best sort – no comparison, the others are hardly eatable.

EMMA (*to* JANE FAIRFAX). Will you accept the governess' post with Mrs Elton's friend?

JANE FAIRFAX. No, not at present.

MRS ELTON. Hautboys very scarce around here – still, chillies are better, abundant in strawberries around Bristol. Maple Grove is swimming in them.

MISS BATES (*to everybody*). I'm sure Frank Churchill will be here soon.

MRS ELTON. The only thing wrong with gathering strawberries is all this stooping. I prefer cherries myself. I can't bear it any longer. I must go and sit in the shade. Now, Jane my dear, come and sit with me. You simply must accept the position as governess you know. I won't hear of you refusing it. We won't hear of you refusing it, will we Mr E?

MR KNIGHTLEY, *who has been talking to* HARRIET, *comes over to* EMMA.

MR KNIGHTLEY. Harriet is a charming young woman. I quite misjudged her.

Soon when MRS ELTON's *attention is diverted,* JANE FAIRFAX *slips away – she comes face to face with* FRANK CHURCHILL – *then rushes off.*

MRS ELTON. Are you ready for my expedition to Box Hill tomorrow, Jane . . . Jane?

Everyone calls to JANE FAIRFAX *and refers to the backstage map to locate her whereabouts.* FRANK CHURCHILL *storms on-stage.*

MRS WESTON. Frank! How are you, my boy?

FRANK CHURCHILL. I am deplorable. The heat is excessive! I wish I were somewhere else. I am sick of England. I wish I were in Switzerland. (EMMA *offers strawberry*.) No, thank you, I do not wish to eat, it will only make me hotter.

EMMA (*to audience*). I am glad I have done being in love with him. I should not like a man who is so soon discomposed by a hot morning. But Harriet's sweet temper will not mind it.

MRS WESTON. We are going to Box Hill tomorrow. It is not Switzerland but it will be something for a young man in want of a change. You will stay and go with us?

FRANK CHURCHILL. No, I shall go home to Richmond in the cool of the evening.

MRS WESTON. But you may come again tomorrow?

FRANK CHURCHILL. No. If I come I shall be cross.

EMMA. Then pray, stay in Richmond.

FRANK CHURCHILL. But if I do, I shall be crosser still. If you wish me to stay and join the party, I will.

NIECE FOUR. And he did.

Scene 25

JANE AUSTEN. Unfortunately, despite all circumstances being in favour of a pleasant party, (*Expectant gasp from party.*) there was a languor, (*Slight deflation.*) a want of spirits, (*More deflation.*) a want of union, (*More deflation.*) which could not be got over. They separated too much into parties.

Everyone separates into parties.

EMMA. This is downright dullness. I have never seen Frank so silent and stupid.

HARRIET. What?

EMMA. Or you.

MRS ELTON. Look at them. (*Points to* EMMA *and* FRANK CHURCHILL.) They are flirting together excessively.

FRANK CHURCHILL (*to* EMMA). Don't say I was cross. The heat overcame me.

EMMA. It is hotter today.

FRANK CHURCHILL. Not of my feelings. Today, I am perfectly comfortable.

EMMA. You are comfortable because you are under command.

FRANK CHURCHILL. Your command? Yes.

EMMA. I meant self-command.

FRANK CHURCHILL. It comes to the same thing. You order me, whether you speak or not. And you can be always with me. You are always with me.

EMMA. Your gallantry is really unanswerable.

FRANK CHURCHILL. I say nothing of which I should be ashamed. I saw you first in February. Let everybody on the hill hear me from Mickleham to Dorking. I saw you first in February. Our companions are being exceedingly stupid. Shall I rouse them for you? Ladies and gentlemen, I am ordered by Miss Woodhouse that she requires something entertaining from each of you. Either one thing clever, two things moderately clever or three things very dull indeed.

MISS BATES. Oh then I need not be too uneasy. That will do just for me, you know. I shall be sure to say three dull things as soon as ever I open my mouth. Do you not all think I shall?

EMMA. There may be a difficulty. You will be limited to only three at once.

EMMA *laughs out loud. Pause as this sinks in.*

MISS BATES. Ah . . . Well to be sure . . . I will try and hold my tongue.

Awkward silence.

MRS ELTON. I protest I must be excused. I am not all fond of this sort of thing. I do not pretend to be a wit. I have a great deal of vivacity in my own way, but I really must be allowed to judge when to speak and when to hold my tongue. Shall we walk?

MR *and* MRS ELTON *walk away.*

FRANK CHURCHILL. Happy couple! How many a man has committed himself on short acquaintance and rued it all the rest of his life.

JANE FAIRFAX. Such things do occur, undoubtedly. A hasty and imprudent attachment may arise – but there is generally time to recover from it afterwards.

FRANK CHURCHILL (*to* EMMA). I do not trust my own judgement. Miss Woodhouse, will you choose a wife for me?

JANE FAIRFAX. Here are the servants with the carriages. It is time to go.

They rise and head for the carriages. As EMMA *is about to get in she is called to one side by* MR KNIGHTLEY.

MR KNIGHTLEY. Emma. How could you be so unfeeling to Miss Bates? How could you be so insolent to a woman of her character, age and situation?

EMMA. Oh, it was not so very bad. I dare say she did not understand me.

MR KNIGHTLEY. I assure you she did. She had spoken of it since. You have laughed at her and humbled her. It was badly done indeed!

MR KNIGHTLEY stalks away. EMMA *in her carriage starts to cry.*

Scene 26

EMMA *sitting on a chair, whilst* JANE AUSTEN *reads from her manuscript.*

JANE AUSTEN. The wretchedness of the scheme to Box Hill was on Emma's thoughts all evening. She must make amends to Miss Bates.

EMMA *gets up and walks to the Bates'.*

NIECE FOUR / SERVANT. The ladies are all at home.

Bustle.

JANE FAIRFAX (*unseen*). Tell her I'm ill.

EMMA. Miss Bates, I . . .

MISS BATES. I am afraid Jane is not very well . . . such a dreadful headache, writing all the morning, such long letters . . . tears in her eyes . . . such a great change in her situation . . . she is amazingly fortunate. Such a fine situation for one so young.

EMMA. Situation?

MISS BATES. She is going as Governess to Mrs Smallridge. Mrs Elton found the post for her. Jane was quite decided against accepting the offer but she changed her mind quite suddenly.

EMMA. And when is Miss Fairfax to leave you?

MISS BATES. Very soon indeed.

EMMA. Miss Bates I . . .

> MISS BATES *exits hurriedly.* EMMA *leaves thoughtfully, walking across the stage. She meets a* NIECE.

NIECE THREE. Good morning, Emma. A pleasant visit?

EMMA. Yes, thank you.

NIECE THREE. Conscience assuaged?

EMMA. Yes. Thank you.

NIECE THREE (*to audience*). Back at Hartfield! . . .

> EMMA *arrives back at her house where* MR WOODHOUSE, MR KNIGHTLEY *and* HARRIET *are seated.*

MR WOODHOUSE. I am very glad indeed my dear to hear Miss Fairfax is to be so comfortably settled.

HARRIET (*greeting* EMMA). Miss Woodhouse.

MR KNIGHTLEY. Emma, I am going to spend a few days in London. But I would not go away without seeing you, (*He is about to take* EMMA*'s hand but* HARRIET *gets in the way.*) but I must leave directly.

> KNIGHTLEY *exits.*

MR WOODHOUSE. I dare say Mrs Elton's acquaintances are just what they ought to be. I hope Miss Fairfax's health will be well taken care of.

> NIECE TWO *rushes downstage screaming.*

NIECE TWO. Mrs Churchill is dead! Mrs Churchill is dead!

> *Other characters talk excitedly amongst themselves.*

MRS WESTON. Poor Mrs Churchill. No doubt she had been suffering a great deal.

EMMA. Yes. Now that she has actually died, we must admit to having slightly misjudged her hypochondria.

MRS WESTON. Poor woman. How will it affect Frank?

EMMA. A sad event indeed . . . of course, an attachment between Frank Churchill and Harriet now has no obstacles to encounter. Harriet must be burning with anticipation.

Scene 27

NIECE TWO. One morning, about ten days after Mrs Churchill's demise, Emma was called downstairs by a messenger.

NIECE ONE. Can you come to Randalls' any time this morning? Mrs Weston must see you.

EMMA. Is she unwell?

NIECE ONE. No, not at all, only a little agitated. Can you come?

EMMA. Certainly, this moment if you please.

They walk out, going to Randalls'.

EMMA. Do let me know what has happened.

NIECE ONE. No. I cannot.

NIECE TWO. What has happened?

NIECE FOUR. What's going on?

NIECE TWO. Is it some disaster?

NIECE FOUR. He's having an affair and his wife has found out . . .

NIECE TWO. His wife's having an affair and he's found out . . .

NIECE FOUR. He's lost all his money in a gaming club . . .

NIECE TWO. Mr Weston and Harriet have run away together . . .

NIECE FOUR. Frank's gone off to help consolidate the French revolution . . .

NIECES (*singing*). Allons enfants de la patrie, Le jour de gloire est arrive!

They are silenced by an extremely black look from JANE
AUSTEN. EMMA *and* NIECES *reach Randalls' where*
MRS WESTON *is waiting, very agitated.* NIECES *depart
to the back of the stage.*

EMMA. What is it my dear friend? Something of a very
unpleasant nature has occurred. Do let me know directly
what it is.

MRS WESTON. Have you indeed no idea?

EMMA. No.

MRS WESTON. Frank has been here this morning and – and –
he and Jane Fairfax have been secretly engaged since
October!

EMMA. Jane Fairfax! Good God! You are not serious?

MRS WESTON. You may well be amazed, but it is even so.
They formed a solemn engagement at Weymouth and kept it
a secret from everybody. I can hardly believe it. I thought
I knew him.

EMMA. Well . . . well . . . well . . .

NIECES *begin to chant quietly,* 'Boyfriend, Boyfriend, yes I
had your boyfriend'.

(*To* NIECES.) Shut up! (*To* JANE AUSTEN.) What on earth
are you playing at? And what about Harriet? She'll be
heartbroken.

NIECE ONE. And what about the things you said to Frank
Churchill about Jane Fairfax?

EMMA *groans and covers her face, walks back to* MRS
WESTON.

EMMA. This is a circumstance, which I must think of at least
half a day before I can at all comprehend it.

MRS WESTON. Oh Emma, it has hurt me very much. Some
part of his conduct we cannot excuse.

EMMA. I will not pretend not to understand you, but please,
be assured that I am not attached to him, despite his
attentions to me.

MRS WESTON. Really?

EMMA. Really. There was a period in the early part of our acquaintance when I did like him and was very much disposed to be attached to him. Fortunately, it ceased. I care nothing about him. This is the simple truth. (*They embrace. MRS WESTON is relieved.*) I have escaped. But that does not acquit him. I think him greatly to blame. What right had he to endeavour to please any one young woman while he really belonged to another? How could Miss Fairfax bear such behaviour?

MRS WESTON. There were misunderstandings between them, Emma, misunderstandings which might possibly have arisen from the impropriety of his conduct.

EMMA. Impropriety! It is too calm a censure. I cannot say how much it has sunk him in my opinion. So unlike what a man should be. None of that upright integrity, that strict adherence to truth and principle which a man should display in every transaction of his life. And Jane actually on the point of being a governess! To suffer her to engage herself. What could he mean by such a horrible indelicacy?

MRS WESTON. He knew nothing about it, Emma. It was the discovery of what she was doing which determined him to come forward at once.

EMMA. Well . . . I supposed we shall gradually grow reconciled to the idea and I wish them very happy. But if by chance Frank Churchill happened to hear any uncomplimentary words spoken about Jane Fairfax, it's his own fault.

Scene 28

EMMA. Poor Harriet! I have done her nothing but disservice. Common sense should have directed me to tell Harriet that there were five hundred chances to one against Frank Churchill ever caring for her – but with common sense, I am afraid I have had little to do.

EMMA *hits herself repeatedly on the head while pacing the stage.*

JANE AUSTEN. She was extremely angry with herself. If she could not have been angry with Frank Churchill, too, it would have been dreadful.

Enter FRANK CHURCHILL *and* JANE FAIRFAX *from opposite ends. They meet in the middle to the music of Piazzolla then exit.*

EMMA. I need no longer be unhappy about Jane. Her days of insignificance and evil are over. She will soon be well and happy and prosperous. But poor Harriet! There is little sympathy to be spared for anybody else. I must communicate that painful truth as . . .

HARRIET enters and interrupts her.

HARRIET. Well, Miss Woodhouse! Is not this the oddest news that ever was!

EMMA. What news do you mean?

HARRIET. That Jane Fairfax and Frank Churchill are to be married!

EMMA (*to audience*). What? No tears?

HARRIET. Had you any idea of his being in love with her? You perhaps might – you who can see into everybody's heart.

EMMA. I begin to doubt my having any such talent. I never had the slightest suspicion. If I had, I should have cautioned you accordingly.

HARRIET. Me! Why should you caution me? You do not think I care about Mr Frank Churchill? You have misunderstood me! I know we agreed never to name him, but considering how infinitely superior he is to everybody, I believed you knew who I meant.

EMMA. Harriet – are you speaking of Mr Knightley?

HARRIET. To be sure I am.

EMMA. Good God! This has been a most unfortunate, most deplorable mistake. What is to be done? Have you any idea of Mr Knightley returning your affection?

HARRIET. Yes, I must say that I have.

NIECES *dash downstage.*

NIECES ONE, TWO *and* THREE. It darted through her, with the speed of an arrow, that Mr Knightley must marry no one but herself.

NIECES *run off and* EMMA *gathers herself.*

EMMA. Pray, Harriet. Do acquaint me with the history of your hopes with Mr Knightley.

HARRIET (*disjointed*). A difference in his behaviour since the two dances – sensible of him talking to me more than he used to – quite a different manner towards me, I cannot recall without a blush – sweetness and kindness. Filled my whole basket with strawberries, Came and walked by me and talked so very delightfully about farming.

EMMA. Is it not possible he might be alluding to Mr Martin? He might have Mr Martin's interest in view.

HARRIET. Mr Martin! No, indeed! I hope I know better now than to care for Mr Martin! I must leave. I am sure you see I have good ground for hope! Goodbye.

EMMA. Oh, God! That I have never seen her. (NIECE *approaches her.*) Get out! (*She shrieks at* NIECES *and is left alone with* JANE AUSTEN.) Humiliating! The blindness of my own head! Wretched. Wretched.

JANE AUSTEN. To understand, thoroughly understand her own heart was the first endeavour.

JANE AUSTEN *sits* EMMA *down.*

EMMA (*in broken sentences*). Mr Knightley so dear to me . . . how long has . . . there's never been a time . . . infinitely superior to Frank Churchill . . . I've never really cared for Frank Churchill at all! (*Pause.*) Except for my affection for Mr Knightley, every other part of my mind is disgusting. (EMMA *stands up, walks to front. House lights up.*) I am insufferably vain, unpardonably arrogant, universally mistaken and full of nothing but mischief. Mr Knightley and Harriet Smith! Such an elevation on her side! Such a debasement on his! Could it be? No, it is impossible. (*To* JANE AUSTEN.) How could Harriet ever have had the presumption to raise her thoughts to Mr Knightley?

JANE AUSTEN. If Harriet from being humble were grown vain, it is your doing and your doing alone.

Elgar's Cello Concerto.

EMMA *breaks down.*

Scene 29

EMMA *is left alone for a long time, finally says to audience:*

EMMA. If I could be secure of Mr Knightley never marrying at all, I should be perfectly satisfied. Marriage, of course, will never do for me. It would be incompatible with what I owe father. Nothing should separate me from father. I will never marry, even if I were asked by Mr Knightley.

MR WOODHOUSE. Emma, my dear! It is a long and melancholy day. There is a cold stormy rain setting in and I can't seem to get comfortable. Could you fetch my rug and the cards and tell cook we will not take supper.

They sit and play cards. JANE AUSTEN *and the* NIECES *gather round.*

JANE AUSTEN. Mr Knightley is to be no longer coming there for his evening comfort. No longer walking in at all hours, as if ever willing to change his own home for theirs. How was it to be endured? If Harriet were to be the chosen, what would increase Emma's wretchedness but the reflection that it had been all her own work?

NIECE ONE. However inferior in spirit and gaiety might be the following (NIECE TWO *joining.*) and every future winter of your life, (NIECE THREE *joining.*) it will yet find you more rational, more acquainted with yourself, (NIECE FOUR *joining.*) and leave you less to regret when it is gone.

Scene 30

NIECE THREE. The next day Emma was taking a turn in the shrubbery when she saw Mr Knightley coming towards her. She had been thinking of him as unquestionably sixteen miles distant. She must be collected and calm.

EMMA. How do you do? When did you leave my sister?

MR KNIGHTLEY. Only this morning.

EMMA. You must have had a wet ride.

MR KNIGHTLEY. Yes.

MR KNIGHTLEY *looks often at* EMMA.

EMMA. Now you are come back, you have some news to hear that will rather surprise you.

MR KNIGHTLEY. Have I? Of what nature?

EMMA. Oh, the best in the world – a wedding.

MR KNIGHTLEY. If you mean Miss Fairfax and Mr Churchill, I have heard that already.

EMMA. Despite your suspicions, I seem to have been doomed to blindness.

MR KNIGHTLEY *takes her arm and presses it to him passionately.*

MR KNIGHTLEY. Time, my dearest Emma, will heal the wound. Abominable scoundrel! He will soon be gone, but Jane Fairfax deserves a better fate.

EMMA. You are very kind, but I am not in want of that sort of compassion.

MR KNIGHTLEY. Oh, Emma! He is no object of regret – he is a disgrace to the name of man. And he is to be rewarded with that sweet young woman. Oh, Jane, Jane, you will be a miserable creature.

EMMA. Mr Knightley, I must make this clear. I have never been at all attached to the person we are speaking of. I was tempted by his attentions, an old story, and no more than has happened to hundreds of my sex before; I found him pleasant. My vanity was flattered. He has imposed on me, but not injured me.

MR KNIGHTLEY *relieved. Pause.*

MR KNIGHTLEY. I have never had a high opinion of Frank Churchill, but with such a woman he has a chance. I wish them well. He is indeed the favour of fortune, everything turns out for his good. He has used everybody ill, and they are all delighted to forgive him.

EMMA. You speak as if you envied him.

MR KNIGHTLEY. I do, Emma. In one respect he is the object of my envy. You will not ask me what is the point of envy. You are wise. But I cannot be wise. Emma, I must tell you what you will not ask, though I may wish it unsaid the next moment.

EMMA. Oh! Then don't speak it, don't speak it! Take a little time, consider, do not commit yourself!

MR KNIGHTLEY. Thank you. (*They reach the house.*) You are going in, I suppose?

EMMA. No, I should like to take another turn. I stopped you ungraciously just now, but if you have any wish to speak openly to me, as a friend, I will hear whatever you like.

MR KNIGHTLEY. As a friend! Emma, that I fear is a word – no – I have no wish. Stay, yes, why should I hesitate? I have gone too far already for concealment. Tell me then, have I no chance of ever succeeding? My dearest Emma, for dearest you will always be, whatever the outcome of this hour's conversation, my dearest beloved Emma, tell me at once. Say no if it is to be said. You are silent! Absolutely silent! At present I ask no more. I cannot make speeches, Emma. If I loved you less I might be able to talk about it more. But you know what I am. You hear nothing but truth from me. I have blamed you, and lectured you and you have borne it as no other woman in England would have borne it. Hear the truth from me now. God knows, I have been an indifferent lover – but you understand me – I ask only once to hear your voice.

NIECES *lean forward in enwrapped anticipation of a kiss.*

MR KNIGHTLEY *and* EMMA *nearly kiss . . .* KNIGHTLEY *pulls away to become* JANE AUSTEN.

JANE AUSTEN. Her way was clear, though not quite smooth. She spoke then, on being so entreated. What did she say? Just what she ought, of course. A lady always does. She said enough to show there need not be despair, and to invite him to say more himself.

NIECE ONE. Oh, that was good of her!

EMMA *and* MR KNIGHTLEY *go hand in hand to the house.*

NIECE TWO. Mr Knightley had found her agitated and low. Frank Churchill was a villain. He had heard her declare that she had never loved him. Mr Knightley's character was not desperate. She was his own Emma, by hand and word, when they returned into the house; and if he could have thought of Frank Churchill then, he might have deemed him a very good sort of fellow.

Scene 31

HARRIET *walks across empty stage, holding mouth, grizzling.*

HARRIET (*to nieces*). I've got a toothache! I'm off to London to visit the dentist.

NIECE TWO. Harriet, have you heard the news?

NIECE THREE. Miss Woodhouse and Mr Knightley are to be married.

NIECES *giggle.* HARRIET *grabs them by their neck and draws them close to her.*

HARRIET. Are they really? Well, I hope they're very happy together. Excuse me, I have a coach to catch.

She pushes NIECES *off, then exits.*

EMMA. Father . . . dearest father . . .

MR WOODHOUSE. What is it, Emma, are you ill? Did the spinach soup give you indigestion? Shall I call for the doctor?

EMMA. Oh, no, no. I'm not ill father. It's just . . . if your consent and approbation could be obtained which I trust it will be with the least amount of difficulty, since it is a plan to promote the happiness of all – Mr Knightley and I mean to marry.

MR WOODHOUSE *is shocked and has a seizure.*

MR WOODHOUSE. You always said you would never marry. It would be a great deal better for you to remain single. Look at poor Isabella and poor Miss Taylor! They married!

EMMA. Father, do you not love Mr Knightley very much? Would you not be glad to see him every day?

MR WOODHOUSE. But we do see him every day as it is. Why can we not go on as we have done?

NIECES *rush in.*

NIECE TWO. A prowler – a prowler! Got all Mrs Weston's turkeys – robbed them, pilfered them. A prowler on the loose!

MR WOODHOUSE. A prowler! A pilferer! A housebreaker! That means a firestarter! (NIECES *all go wild – few bars of 'Firestarter' from the Prodigy.*) I shall be under the most wretched alarm every night of my life.

EMMA. Except if Mr Knightley were here.

MR WOODHOUSE. Of course the wedding must be sooner rather than later, Emma, so Mr Knightley can stay and look after me. I mean there is no point in putting these things off. Within the month I should say!

Big cheer from the nieces.

Enter JANE FAIRFAX *and* FRANK CHURCHILL.

JANE FAIRFAX. I have received a telegram from France. Proust would like me to join him in Paris to discuss my critical work on 'Remembrance Of Times Past.' It won't interfere too much with our honeymoon, will it, my love?

HARRIET (*to* ROBERT MARTIN). My new threshing machine will then sift the grain and store it, making it doubly economical. Do you see, Robert? We shall spend our honeymoon at Agricultural College. And where will you spend yours, Emma?

EMMA. Happy as I am for all of you, I cannot possibly leave Highbury. There is so much to do.

ALL. Like what?

EMMA. Well, the new Squire's daughter needs introducing into polite society and the shrubbery needs pruning.

Then all dance to music of 'Scottish Reform Jig'. MRS ELTON *cuts music.*

MRS ELTON. A very poor wedding. Very little white satin. Very few lace veils. A most pitiful business. Poor Knightley, poor fellow. She had always meant to catch Knightley if she could. What a sad business. How could he be so taken in? He is obviously not in the least in love. No more exploring parties to Donwell made for me. Oh no! There will be a Mrs Knightley to throw cold water on everything.

MRS ELTON *begins music again and they finish the dance.*

MISS BATES. You may kiss the bride.

All couples kiss.

Bells.

Confetti.

The End.